GREAT ISLAMIC

Averroes

RELATED TITLES PUBLISHED BY ONEWORLD

Muslim Women Mystics: The Life of Rabi'a and other Women Mystics in Islam, Margaret Smith, ISBN 1–85168–250–3

Faith and Reason in Islam: Averroes's Exposition of Religious Arguments, Ibrahim Najjar, ISBN 1–85168–263–5

Rumi – Past and Present, East and West: The Life, Teachings and Poetry of Jalâl al-Din Rumi, Franklin D. Lewis, ISBN 1–85168–241–7

GREAT ISLAMIC THINKERS

Averroes

(Ibn Rushd)

His Life, Works and Influence

MAJID FAKHRY

ONEWORLD

OXFORD

AVERROES: HIS LIFE, WORKS AND INFLUENCE

Oneworld Publications
(Sales and Editorial)
185 Banbury Road
Oxford OX2 7AR
England
www.oneworld-publications.com

ISBN 1–85168–269–4

Cover design by Design Deluxe
Typeset by LaserScript Ltd, Mitcham, UK
Printed and bound in India by Replika Press Pvt. Ltd.

Cover picture: *The School of Athens*, detail from the left hand side showing Pythagoras surrounded by students and Michelangelo, 1510-11 (fresco) (detail of 472) by Raphael (Raffaello Sanzio of Urbino) (1483-1520). © Vatican Museums and Gallaries, Vatican City, Italy/Bridgeman Art Library.
Averroes appears standing behind Pythagoras and looking over his shoulder.

Contents

Preface

Abu'l-Walīd Ibn Rushd, better known as Averroes (1126–1198), stands out
as a towering figure in the history of Arab–Islamic thought, as well as that
of West-European philosophy and theology. In the Arab–Islamic world, he
played a decisive role in the defense of Greek philosophy against the
onslaughts of the Ash'arite theologians (Mutakallimun), led by al-Ghazālī
(d. 1111), and the rehabilitation of Aristotle. In the Western world, he was
recognized, as early as the thirteenth century, as the *Commentator* of
Aristotle, contributing thereby to the rediscovery of the Master, after
centuries of near-total oblivion in Western Europe. That discovery was
instrumental in launching Latin Scholasticism and, in due course, the
European Renaissance of the fifteenth century. Notwithstanding, there has
been very little attention to Averroes' work in English, although greater
interest has been shown in French, since the publication of Ernest Rénan's
outstanding *Averroès et l'averroïsme* in 1852, and since that time in Spanish.

I have tried in this volume to give a comprehensive account of
Averroes' contribution to the fields of Aristotelian exegesis, Islamic
theology, jurisprudence and medicine. In addition, I have tried to
highlight his impact on European thought, both Jewish and Christian, and
the reception of his philosophy in the Islamic world. In the final chapter, I
have dealt with the encounter of Averroes and Aquinas, the two greatest
Aristotelians in the thirteenth century.

Unless otherwise indicated, translations in the text are mine.

In closing, I wish to express my appreciation to Oneworld and its Director, Novin Doostar, for including this volume in their new series, Great Islamic Thinkers, and to the Center for Muslim-Christian Understanding at Georgetown University for permission to reproduce parts of my paper, "Averroes, Aquinas and the Rediscovery of Aristotle in Western Europe", published by that Center in 1997.

Majid Fakhry
September 2000

Introduction

The Hellenistic phase in the history of Greek philosophy coincided with the founding of Alexandria in Egypt by Alexander the Great in 332 B.C.E. From that time on, Alexandria became the heiress of Athens as the cultural center of the ancient world, especially in the fields of the positive sciences and medicine. In philosophy, that phase was marked by its syncretism and its tendency to bring together Greek, Chaldean, Egyptian, Phoenician, Jewish and Christian elements, culminating, in the second and third centuries of the Christian era, in Neoplatonism, the last great monument of Greek philosophy.

The accredited founder of this philosophy was Plotinus, who was born in Lycopolis, Egypt, in 205, and died in Rome in 270. His teaching was continued in the Near East and beyond by his disciple and editor, Porphyry of Tyre (d. 303), Jamblichus (d. 385), Syrian disciple of Porphyry, and in turn by Jamblichus' disciple, Proclus of Athens (d. 485), the last great proponent of Greek paganism. Shortly after, the eclipse of Greek philosophy in its homeland and the rest of Europe began, when the Byzantine emperor, Justinian, ordered the School of Athens, which was the last bastion of Greek paganism, to be closed. Seven of its teachers, led by Simplicius (fl. 533), crossed into Persia, lured by reports of the philhellenic sympathies of the Persian emperor, Chosroes I, known in Arabic sources as Anūshirwan or the Just. This episode heralded the eastward migration of Greek philosophy, which the afore-mentioned Hellenistic or Alexandrian phase had inaugurated.

The next historic phase in the history of Greek philosophy was the Arab–Islamic, which began during the Abbasid period (750–1258), when Baghdad, the Abbasid capital, inherited from Alexandria and Athens the title of cultural center of the world. Philosophers, scientists and theologians converged on it from all the corners of the Islamic world.

The first of those philosophers–scientists was al-Kindī (d. c. 866), who wrote on the whole range of ancient learning from logic, to arithmetic, psychology, meteorology, astrology and metaphysics. Al-Kindī lived during a period of profound soul-searching, during which the theological rationalists, known as Mu'tazilites, were pitted against their arch-rivals, the Ḥanbalites, the Malikites and other traditionalists, who rejected the application of rational methods of discourse, borrowed from the Greeks, as tantamount to heresy (*bid'ah*) or irreligion (*kufr*).

Al-Kindī, who sympathized with the Mu'tazilite desire to rationalize Islamic dogma, faced the traditionalists with singular determination and ensured thereby a secure, if short-lived, foothold for philosophy in Muslim lands. His successors, including al-Fārābī (d. 950) and Ibn Sīnā, also known as Avicenna (d. 1037), faced the same challenges in the next two centuries and developed in the process a metaphysical world-view, grounded in Neoplatonism, which they believed to be compatible with the Islamic system of beliefs. Their position was soon challenged by the new school of theology (*kalām*), which stemmed originally from Mu'tazilism itself. Its founder, Abū'l-Ḥasan al-Ash'ari (d. 935), an ex-Mu'tazilite, favored the application of theological methods of proof to Islamic dogmas, but was inclined to agree with the traditionalists, including Ibn Ḥanbal (d. 855), on the substance of their dogmatic teaching. His followers, who constitute a galaxy of outstanding theologians, or Mutakallimun, included al-Bāqillāni (d. 1012), al-Baghdādi (d. 1037), al-Juwayni (d. 1086) and his disciple al-Ghazālī, generally regarded as the greatest theologian or Proof of Islam (*Hujjat al-Islām*).

Al-Ghazālī was thoroughly schooled in the ways of the philosophers, as his *Intentions of the Philosophers*, his *Criterion of Knowledge* (or logic) and his

Balance of Action (or ethics) clearly show. His sympathies, however, were thoroughly religious and mystical, and thus he bent all his energies to the rebuttal of those parts of Greek philosophy, which "were in conflict with the fundamentals of religion," according to him. These consisted of the bulk of physical and metaphysical propositions, that the Muslim Neoplatonists, led by al-Farābī and Avicenna, had popularized. Significantly enough, unlike the majority of other theologians, he regarded the other branches of philosophy, such as logic, ethics and mathematics, as entirely innocuous from a religious point of view.

Be this as it may, al-Ghazālī's onslaught on Greek–Arabic philosophy, embodied chiefly in his *Tahāfut al-Falāsifah* (Incoherence of the Philosophers), is a landmark in the history of the confrontation of the theologians and the philosophers of Islam. At a time when the Muslim world was racked with strife between the Shi'ite Fātimids of Egypt and the Sunnite Abbasids of Baghdad, the theological battle was deemed as crucial as the political and military battle. Al-Ghazālī was the standard-bearer of the struggle against the philosophical and Shi'ite party, who had been from the start strange bedfellows. In fact, the Shi'ite or Ismā'ili pro-philosophical sympathies dated back to the tenth century, which witnessed the rise of a popular philosophical fraternity at Basrah, known as the Brethren of Purity.

Al-Ghazālī's onslaught in the eleventh century may be said to have signaled the death of philosophy in the East, but it soon gained a new lease of life in the West. Starting in the ninth century during the reign of Muḥammad ibn 'Abd al-Raḥmān (852–886), the study of mathematical and juridical subjects appears to have prepared the ground for the study of the so-called 'ancient sciences,' during the reign of al-Ḥakam II, known as al-Mustanṣir Billāh (961–976). This enlightened prince ordered the importation of books from the East, to such a point that Cordova, the capital of Muslim Spain (al-Andalus), soon began to rival Baghdad as the center of learning, with its famous library which housed some 400,000 books. However, the picture changed with the accession of al-Ḥakam's son, Hishām (976–1009), who reversed the cultural policies of his father and ordered the books of 'ancient learning' to be burned, with the exception of astronomy, logic and arithmetic, in an attempt to appease the jurists and the masses at large, generally inclined to accuse the adepts of such subjects as downright heretics or infidels.

During the reign of the successor Berber dynasties, the fate of these sciences, including philosophy and theology, or *kalām*, did not change perceptibly. The first of these dynasties, al-Murābitūn (Almoravids), who ruled Spain and North Africa from 1090 to 1147, adhered to a rigid form of the Maliki legal creed (*madhhab*), and encouraged the study of jurisprudence (*fiqh*), but prohibited the study of theology (*kalām*) and the 'ancient sciences,' including philosophy. In that respect, they were following in the footsteps of the founder of the Maliki school, Mālik Ibn Anas (d. 795), who had no use for rational discourse of any kind. Asked once about the Qur'anic verses which speak of God's sitting on the throne (*istiwā*'), he is reported to have replied: "The sitting is well-known, its modality is unknown; belief in it is obligatory and questioning it is a heresy (*bid'ah*)."

With the advent of the Muwaḥḥidūn (Almohades) in 1146, the intellectual climate in al-Andalus and North Africa changed somewhat. The founder of the Almohades dynasty, Aḥmad Ibn Tumart (d. 1128), introduced the study of theology (*kalām*), and this opened the way for the study of philosophy and the 'ancient sciences,' which had been neglected in the West, as we have seen. It is to be noted that Ibn Tumart was somewhat eclectical in his approach to *kalām*, since he favored the Mu'tazilite method on some questions and the Ash'arite method on other questions. In law, he remained a Zahirite, following in the footsteps of Ibn Ḥazm (d. 1068), and thus regarded Scripture (*shar*') as the final authority in matters of religious law (*sharī'ah*) and ritual observances (*'ibādāt*), as well.

However, despite his profession of the Maliki creed, Ibn Tumart believed that the apparent conflict between *kalām* and philosophy can be resolved by recourse to the intuitive principles of reason, which stipulate that every action or occurrence should be referred to an Agent, as the principle of causality and the Qur'an itself stipulate, in such verses as 11: 14 and 11: 17, which refer to the Qur'an as a revelation from God and "a clear proof from their Lord." It follows that upon this as a premise, Ibn Tumart held, we can prove the existence of God, and thus "it is certain that God Almighty can be known through the necessity of reason," as he has put it in his best known work, the *Dearest Quest* (*A'azz mā Yuṭlab*).[1] He then inveighs against those who claim that the religious law (*sharī'ah*) is incompatible with wisdom or philosophy (*ḥikmah*), "demeaning thereby religion itself and ignoring God's wisdom."[2] He was also convinced, like Averroes, who is known to have written a *Commentary on Ibn Tumart's Creed*, that deduction (*qiyās*), whether religious (*shar'ī*) or rational (*'aqlī*) is the pathway to certainty, contrary to 'conjectural' deductions which have led many sectarians, such as the Non-attributionists (Mu'attilah) and the Corpore-alists (Mujassimah), astray. He was also convinced that rational and legal deductions are equivalent; for in the case of the former, we distinguish between the necessary, the possible and the impossible; whereas in the case of the latter, we distinguish between the obligatory, the lawful and the unlawful – the two sets of categories being analogous, according to him.

In further defending this view, Ibn Tumart goes on to argue that legal deduction, which has five varieties, was actually used by the different sects, including the already-mentioned Non-attributionists, the Corpore-alists and others, in support of their specious propositions. The five varieties are then given by him as follows:

1. The existential deduction, which has led the Corporealists to infer from what is an object of empirical observation that the Creator Himself must be corporeal.
2. The habitual deduction, which led some to hold that all existing entities are generated by other existing entities, so that a being who does not generate other existing entities, similar to him, does not exist – from which they inferred that God does not exist.
3. The observational deduction, according to which everything we observe must exist in a given locus. It follows, then, that God Himself must exist in a locus.
4. The active deduction, from which some have inferred that whoever is responsible for a certain action, such as injustice or aggression, must be described as an unjust aggressor. From this premise they inferred that God must be so described.

1. *A'azz mā Yuṭlab*, p. 214.
2. *Ibid.*, p. 157.

5. The causal deduction, which stipulates, on the basis of observation, that the knowledge subsisting in the knower is the cause of his being a knower. Ibn Tumart objects to this type of deduction on the ground that, if this were the case, God's knowledge would be contingent, rather than necessary, and thus knowledge could be denied of Him.[3]

This interest in defining rational deduction, as distinct from legal deduction, and its many varieties, will play a decisive role in Averroes' attempt to demonstrate the harmony of religion (*Sharī'ah*) and philosophy (*ḥikmah*) in his *Decisive Treatise*, as will appear in due course, by highlighting the analogy between the two varieties of deduction, the religious, used by the jurists and the theologians and the rational, used by the philosophers.

Although the Almoravids, as we have mentioned, were averse to the study of philosophy, theology and the 'ancient sciences,' it is noteworthy that they do not appear to have actively combated this study. This is illustrated by the fact that the beginnings of philosophical speculation in al-Andalus coincide with the latter part of their rule. Thus, of the earliest scholars, the Andalusian historian, Ṣā'id (d. 1070) mentions Maslamah Ibn Ahmad al-Majrīti (d. 1008), who distinguished himself in astronomy and the occult sciences, and is said to have traveled in the East and brought back with him to Spain the *Epistles of the Brethren of Purity.* According to other reports, these were brought to Spain by his disciple, al-Kirmāni.[4]

Other scholars who cultivated interest in philosophy and the 'ancient sciences' are mentioned by Ṣā'id. They included Ibn al-Nabbāsh al-Bajjā'i, Abu'l-Fadl Ibn Hasdai, Ahmad Ibn Hafṣūn, nicknamed the philosopher, and others. An earlier Andalusian scholar, Muḥammad Ibn 'Abdullah Ibn Masarrah (d. 931), is said to have inclined to Mu'tazilite theology and mysticism, and if we are to believe the Spanish Orientalist, Asín Palacios, a form of apocryphal Empedoclean doctrine.[5]

However, the first genuine philosopher of al-Andalus was Abū Bakr Ibn al-Sāyigh, better known as Ibn Bājjah or Avempace (d. 1138). Unlike

---

3. *Ibid.*, pp. 158 f.
4. Ṣā'id al-Andalusi, *Tabaqāt al-Uman*, pp. 80 f.
5. *Ibid.*, pp. 21 f. Cf. Asín Palacios, *Ibn Masarra y su escuela.*

his Andalusian predecessors mentioned above, Avempace was thoroughly versed in philosophy, logic and medicine. He wrote paraphrases of Aristotle's *Physics, Meteorology, Generation and Corruption,* the *Book of Animals,* as Aristotle's zoological corpus was called in Arabic, and the spurious *De Plantis.* In addition, he wrote extensive glosses (*ta'āliq*) on the logical works of al-Farābi, for whom he had the highest regard, in addition to an original political treatise, modeled on al-Farābi's *Virtuous City* and entitled the *Conduct of the Solitary (Tadbīr al-Mutawaḥḥid)*.

The second major figure in the history of Andalusian philosophy was Abū Bakr Ibn Ṭufayl (d. 1185), a close friend and associate of Averroes. His only extant work, *Ḥayy Ibn Yaqzān,* is a philosophical novel which embodies the substance of Islamic Neoplatonism, tempered by certain Sufi tendencies, which al-Ghazālī had popularized in the East.

The pivotal figure in the history of Andalusian philosophy, however, was Abū'l-Walīd Muḥammad Ibn Aḥmad Ibn Rushd, better known in European sources as Averroes, on whom the present study centers. Averroes' philosophy marks the climactic point in the development of Arab–Islamic philosophy and the conclusion of four centuries of philosophical–theological warfare in Islam. In global cultural terms, his contribution to Aristotelian scholarship marks a critical point in the history of the transmission of Greek–Arabic philosophy to Western Europe, at a time when Greek philosophy in general and Aristotelianism in particular had been almost completely forgotten in the West. For, with the exception of the translation of Aristotle's logical works by Boethius (d. 525) and parts of Plato's *Timaeus* by Chalcidus (fourth century), very little of Greek philosophy had survived in the West. Thus, when Averroes' commentaries on Aristotle were translated into Latin early in the thirteenth century, they caused a profound intellectual stir in philosophical and theological circles in Western Europe, and laid the groundwork for the rise of Latin Scholasticism, which prior to the rediscovery of Aristotle, thanks chiefly to Averroes' commentaries, would have been inconceivable. Even the rise of Renaissance rationalism and humanism is closely linked to Averroes' commitment to the primacy of reason in philosophical and theological discourse. Thus, as Etienne Gilson has written in his *Reason and Revelation in the Middle Ages,* "Rationalism was born in Spain in the mind of an Arabian philosopher, as a conscious reaction against the theologism of the Arabian divines," by whom he means the Ash'arite Mutakallimun. He then adds that when Averroes died in 1198, "he bequeathed to his successors the ideal of a purely rational philosophy, an ideal whose influence was to be such that, by it even the evolution of Christian philosophy was to be deeply modified."[6] In this respect, it can be argued that Averroes' 'philosophical rationalism' is not only five centuries earlier, but even more comprehensive than the 'mathematical rationalism' of René Descartes (d. 1650), generally regarded as the father of modern philosophy.

Apart from his contribution to the philosophical and theological debate which ripped the intellectual world of Islam apart, Averroes is the only Muslim philosopher to have taken an active interest in the juridical debate of the time in al-Andalus. He served as the religious judge (*qāḍī*) of Seville (1169–1172), chief judge of Cordova (1172–1182), and in 1182 was appointed physician royal at the court of Marrakesh. He also wrote a number of juridical treatises of which only the *Primer of the Discretionary Scholar (Bidāyat al-Mujtahid)* has survived. In this treatise, Averroes explains that his aim is to discuss those juridical decisions which are the subject of consensus or dissension among scholars and to determine their bases in the explicit statement of Scripture (*shar'*). Here his vast erudition in the field of jurisprudence is revealed, since he mentions, then discusses, every juridical opinion, liberal or conservative, Hanafi, Shafi, Māliki or Ḥanbali, and does not always stick to the Māliki opinion, despite his official status as a Māliki judge.

In addition to jurisprudence, philosophy and theology, Averroes contributed extensively to medicine, to which he devoted a large number of treatises, the most famous of which is *al-Kulliyat*, translated into Latin as *Colliget*, together with a number of medical tracts, many of which have survived. They consist mostly of epitomes or summaries (*talākhīs*) of some of Galen's medical works. To these tracts should be added a commentary on Avicenna's famous medical poem, *al-Urjūzah fi'l-Ṭibb*, which has also survived in Arabic and Latin.

---

6. *Reason and Revelation in the Middle Ages*, p. 37.

1

Life and Works

According to his leading biographers, including al-Marākushi (d. 1224), Ibn al-Abbār (d. 1260), Ibn Abī Uṣaybiʻah (d. 1270) and al-Anṣāri (d. 1288), Averroes was born in Cordova, Spain, in 1126, into a prominent family of religious (Māliki) judges and statesmen, and in the manner of his father and grandfather, who served as Māliki judges of Cordova, the young Averroes studied jurisprudence, Arabic, letters (*adab*), theology (*kalām*), philosophy and medicine at the hands of a number of teachers whose names are sometimes mentioned by his biographers. Thus, of his medical teachers, Abū Jaʼfar Hārūn and Abū Marwān Ibn Jurbul of Valencia are mentioned by name, but his closest medical associate was the famous Abū Bakr Ibn Zuhr, who died in 1162. None of Averroes' philosophy teachers are mentioned by name, but he appears to have been influenced by Avempace, who was responsible for introducing the study of Aristotle into al-Andalus, as we have seen, and for whom Averroes had the highest regard. He was, in addition, a close friend of Ibn Ṭufayl, who served as physician royal of the caliph, Abū Yaʻqūb Yusūf, who appears to have been genuinely interested in philosophy. Ibn Ṭufayl's 'illuminationist' (*Ishrāqi*) or mystical sympathies cannot have appealed much to Averroes, who was highly critical of the *Ishrāqi* tendencies of Avicenna and the Sufi tendencies of al-Ghazālī, whose thought was at the heart of Ibn Ṭufayl's philosophical outlook. However, Averroes' association with Ibn Ṭufayl proved very fruitful in determining the direction of his philosophical output; since it was Ibn Ṭufayl who introduced him to the caliph in 1169, commending him "for his acumen, his sound instinct and his attachment to the art (of philosophy)." Whereupon, we are told by the historian al-Marākushi, the caliph addressed to him the question: "What' do the philosophers believe regarding heaven? Is it eternal or created in time (*ḥādith*)?" In response, Averroes, thoroughly taken aback, denied that he was "engaged in the study of philosophy." To allay his fears, the caliph then proceeded to expound the views of Plato, Aristotle and the other philosophers on this question, as well as the objections of Muslim scholars to these views. "I found in him [i.e. the caliph] a profuseness of learning I did not suspect in specialists in that field," Averroes later told one of his disciples.[1]

It was chiefly as a result of this encounter of the philosopher and the prince that Averroes' philosophical career was launched. For that prince, an avid reader of Aristotle, had complained to Ibn Ṭufayl about "the obscurity of Aristotle's idiom or that of his translators" and expressed the wish that he might attempt an interpretation of the philosopher's works for his use. Already advanced in years, Ibn Ṭufayl excused himself and recommended Averroes, whose talents he greatly admired, as we have seen. From that time on, Averroes' career as the Commentator began, since his earliest Aristotelian works, the paraphrases of the *Parts of Animals*, the *Generation of Animals* and the *Parva Naturalia* (*al-Ḥiss wa'l Maḥsūs*) were written in the same year, 1169.

When Abū Yusūf Ya'qūb, nicknamed al-Manṣūr, succeeeded his father in 1184, Averroes continued to enjoy the same royal patronage; but in 1195, probably in response to public pressure instigated by the Māliki jurists, who were averse to the study of philosophy and the 'ancient sciences,' the fortunes of Averroes took an adverse turn. According to other accounts given by Averroes' biographers, a variety of charges appear to have been leveled at the philosopher. Thus, Ibn Abī Uṣaybi'ah attributed his disgrace to his reference to al-Manṣūr, in the *Book of Animals*, as the 'king of the Berbers' (*al-barbar*), which could also be construed in

1. Al-Marākushi, *al-Mu'jib*, pp. 174 f.

Arabic as the Barbarians. Al-Ansāri attributes it to his statement elsewhere, in connection with the People of 'Ād and the wind which destroyed them, as mentioned in Qu'ran 54:19: "Indeed, the existence of the People of 'Ād is uncertain; what then of the news of their destruction" by that wind?[2] Finally, al-Marākushi attributes Averroes' disgrace to his reference to Venus as one of the Gods.[3]

The writings of Averroes covered a greater variety of subjects, philosophical, medical, juridical and linguistic than those of any of his predecessors in the East. However, by far the largest part of his output consisted of commentaries or paraphrases of all the works of Aristotle, with the exception of the *Politics*, for which he substituted the *Republic* of Plato. The commentaries are usually divided into large (*tafsīr*), intermediate (*sharḥ*) and short, i.e. paraphrase or epitomes (*jawāmi'*). It is noteworthy that the only works of Aristotle on which Averroes wrote all three types of commentaries or paraphrases are the *Physics*, the *Metaphysics, De Anima, De Coelo* and *Analytica Posteriora*. In addition, he wrote commentaries on *De Intellectu* of Alexander of Aphrodisias, the *Metaphysics* of Nicolaus of Damascus, the *Isagoge* of Porphyry and the *Almajest* of Ptolemy.

To these commentaries or paraphrases should be added a series of original philosophical writings, some of which have survived in Arabic, Hebrew or Latin. They include treatises *On the Intellect, On the Syllogism, On Conjunction with the Active Intellect, On Time, On the Heavenly Sphere* and *On the Motion of the Sphere*. A number of polemical treatises, some of which have also survived, include an *Essay on al-Fārābī's Approach to Logic, as Compared to that of Aristotle, Metaphysical Questions Dealt with in the Book of Healing (al-Shifā')* by Ibn Sīnā and a *Rebuttal of Ibn Sīnā's Classification of Existing Entities into Possible Absolutely, Possible in Themselves but Necessary by Another and Necessary in Themselves*.[4]

Averroes' theological works consist of a trilogy, which begins with the *Incoherence of the Incoherence (Tahāfut al-Tahāfut)* (1180), a rebuttal of

2. Rénan, *Averroès*, Appendix, pp. 444, 452.
3. Al-Marākushi, *al-Mu'jib*, p. 175.
4. For a list of the commentaries, see Wolfson, "Revised Plan for the Publication of a Corpus Commentariorum Averrois in Aristotelem," pp. 90 f. Cf. Rénan, *Averroès*, pp. 58 f. Cf. also Ibn Abi Usaybi'ah, *'Uyūn al-Anbā*, pp. 23 f.

al-Ghazālī's own *Incoherence of the Philosophers* (*Tahāfut al-Falāsifah*), the *Decisive Treatise on the Relation of Philosophy and Religion* (*Faṣl al-Maqāl*) (1178) and the *Exposition of the Methods of Proof* (*al-Kashf 'an Manāhij al-Adillah*) (1179), to which should be added a short *Appendix* (*Ḍamīmah*) on the nature of God's knowledge, and a lost tract, entitled *That Which the Peripatetics and the Theologians of our Religion* (*al-Mutakallimun*) *Believe with Respect to the Manner of the World's Existence is Close in Meaning*.

His juridical writings include a *Prolegomena, al-Mustaṣfa* (*Gist of Jurisprudence*) and the *Primer of the Discretionary Scholar* (*Bidāyat al-Mujtahid*) (1168), which has survived.

In medicine, as already mentioned in the Introduction, Averroes' major medical treatise is *al-Kulliyāt* (1162), known in Latin translation as *Colliget*, to which should be added short tracts *On Fever, On the Humours, On Theriac*, plus a long list of summaries or paraphrases of Galen's medical treatises and, finally, a commentary on Avicenna's medical poem *al-Urjūzah* (1179–80). These works will be discussed in a later chapter.

The list closes with a grammatical and a linguistic treatise, neither of which has survived.

2

Averroes and the Muslim
Neoplatonists

Rehabilitation of Aristotle

In his attempt to rehabilitate Aristotle, Averroes begins by mounting a
sustained attack against the Muslim Neoplatonists, led by al-Fārābī and
Avicenna, on the double charge that they either distorted or
misunderstood his teaching. Although Averroes does not mention it
explicitly, those philosophers had been misled by the peculiar historical
circumstance that Aristotle's teaching had been confused with that of
Plotinus, sometimes referred to in the Arabic sources as the Greek Sage
(*al-Shaykh al-Yunāni*), as well as that of Proclus, the last great Greek
exponent of Neoplatonism. In the case of the former, a paraphrase of the
last three books of his *Enneads*, due probably to his disciple and editor,
Porphyry of Tyre, was translated into Arabic by 'Abd al-Masīh Ibn
Nā'imah al-Himsi (d. 835), under the rubric of *Āthulugia Aristotālis*,
Theologia Aristotelis, or *Kitāb al-Rubūbiyah* (the Book of Divinity). In the case
of the latter, excerpts from his *Elements of Theology* were translated into
Arabic in the tenth century, as *Fi' l Khayr al-Mahd*, (on the Pure Good),
known in Latin translation as *Liber de causis*, and wrongly attributed to
Aristotle, too.[1]

---

1. Cf. M. Fakhry, *A History of Islamic Philosophy*, pp. 19 f.

Of the two pseudo-Aristotelian treatises, the former was by far the most influential in shaping the thinking of the Muslim Neoplatonists, and it is significant that almost all the early philosophers, from al-Kindī to al-Fārābī and Avicenna, accepted it without question as a genuine work of Aristotle. Even philosophers as late as al-Shirāzi (d. 1641) continue to refer to it as an Aristotelian treatise and quote it extensively in that spirit. Nowhere, as far as I am aware, does Averroes himself refer to either of these alleged Aristotelian treatises, due to an instinctive suspicion, perhaps, that these two works were spurious.

In his critique of Muslim Neoplatonism, Averroes begins by taking al-Fārābī to task, for his misguided attempt to bring Plato and Aristotle together, in his well-known treatise, the *Reconciliation of Two Sages* (*al-Jam'*), which appears to have some relation to a lost treatise of Porphyry of Tyre, mentioned in the Suidas, *Lexicon* II. In the *Epitome of the Metaphysics*, Averroes argues that Aristotle diverged from his master on a variety of points, the most important of which being the latter's view of universals (or Ideas). According to this view, Ideas subsist in a world of their own, known for that reason as the World of Ideas. The existence of those Ideas, according to Aristotle, cannot be demonstrated and is not, at any rate, very helpful in explaining the particulars of sense or even proving their existence. The arguments of the Platonists in support of their view of the nature or status of the Ideas, according to Averroes, are not convincing and are in fact reducible to "poetic and enigmatic discourses used in teaching the general public," rather than the learned.[2] Significantly enough, Averroes does not dwell in his extant works on any of the other arguments advanced by al-Fārābī in his attempt to reconcile the two masters, such as his contention that Plato and Aristotle were at one in their view that the world is created in time, their respective theories of vision, the survival of the soul after death, the nature of ethical traits and so on.

Averroes was equally critical of al-Fārābī's approach to logic, as compared with that of Aristotle, as shown by his already-mentioned logical tract, which is lost, and another tract which had a more specific

---

2. Jawāmi mā ba'd al-Tabi'ah, in *Rasā'il Ibn Rushd*, pp. 48 and 56.

intent; namely, al-Fārābī's divergence from Aristotle in his *Kitāb al-Burhan* (*the Book of Demonstration*), or paraphrase of Aristotle's *Analytica Posteriora*. In his extant logical works, Averroes often disputes al-Fārābī's interpretation of Aristotle's logic, as will appear in a later chapter, and from the already-mentioned treatise criticizing al-Fārābī's approach to logic, as distinct from Aristotle's approach.[3]

Critique of Avicennian Emanationism

More wide-ranging is Averroes' critique of Avicenna, with whose name Islamic Neoplatonism was identified in the Middle Ages in both East and West. He asserts, in this context, that the theory of emanation, which forms the cornerstone of Neoplatonism, is "something which the old company (*al-qawm*) (meaning Aristotle and his followers) knew nothing about," but was popularized by al-Fārābī, Avicenna and their followers, "who so completely distorted the teaching of the ancients in the science of metaphysics that it has become purely conjectural."[4]

The fallacies inherent in the emanationist view, Averroes continues, are legion. Its proponents have arrived at it by recourse to the strange gambit of comparing 'the Invisible Agent,' i.e. God, to the visible, from which they drew the illicit inference that the Invisible Agent, whom they refer to as the One or First, produces a single entity, called the first intellect, or Nous, as Plotinus had called it. From the first intellect a second intellect emanates, and then a third, until we reach the tenth or the Active Intellect, as it was called. This view rests on a false analogy between God and visible agents, who can only operate in a uniform and limited manner; since it entails that God's mode of operation is equally uniform and limited. As the Supreme Agent, God can certainly operate in a variety of ways for which there is no parallel in the visible world. Thus, He can bring simple or compound entities into being, as He pleases.[5]

Moreover, the whole Neoplatonic account of the way in which multiplicity or plurality arises is tenuous; it rests on the premise that, in

3. *Supra*, p. xx.
4. *Tahāfut al-Tahāfut*, p. 182.
5. *Ibid.*, pp. 180 f.

apprehending itself as possible in itself, the first intellect generates the first heaven, and in apprehending itself as necessary through the One or First, it generates the second intellect, which, in turn, generates the third intellect and so on, until we reach the Active Intellect. Aristotle's genuine teaching, Averroes argues, is that in the act of apprehension, the subject and the object are identified, and thus plurality is reduced to unity, especially where the immaterial intellects of Neoplatonic cosmology are concerned.

Moreover, for Aristotle, the existence of compound entities is bound up with the principle of their composition or coming together, "so that the giver of composition (*ribāt, tarkīb*) is the cause of existence." This is particularly true of the ultimate composition of matter and form, which is characteristic of all entities which exist in the world of generation and corruption.[6]

For Avicenna, it will be recalled, the act of generating or bringing material entities into being is tantamount to the act of causing the 'substantial forms,' emanating from the Active Intellect, to inhere in their material substrata. This occurs when they become 'disposed' for their reception, under the influence of terrestrial and celestial agents. It is for this reason that Avicenna refers to the Active Intellect, which is the repository of all forms, whether material or immaterial, as the Giver of Forms (*Wahīb al-Ṣuwar*).[7] The logical corollary of this view, according to Averroes, is to rob all actual entities of any active powers, and to deny, in the manner of the Ash'arites, the principle of causal efficacy.

Averroes next subjects the Avicennian thesis, that existence is an accident superadded to essence, to a searching critique. Instead of regarding existence as the constitutive principle of any given entity, it is represented as an extraneous factor, which upon being superadded to essence, brings that essence into being. This view is reminiscent of Plato's theory of Ideas, according to which the existence of essences, or Ideas, is prior to that of the particulars corresponding to them. For both Aristotle and Averroes, the reverse is true; existence is prior to essence, which is arrived at by a process of abstraction, once the existence of the entity

6. *Ibid.*, pp. 180 f. and 152. Cf. *Tafsīr* III, p. 1498.
7. Ibn Sīnā, *Kitāb al-Najāt*, p. 319.

corresponding to it has been ascertained. Avicenna was guilty of this fallacy, according to Averroes, because he confused the terms one and being; the former is an accident predicable of the ten categories, but not the latter. In the *Large Commentary on the Metaphysics,* Averroes writes: "Avicenna believes that existence and one refer to the same aspect of the thing superadded to its essence. He does not believe that the thing exists, *per se,* but rather through an adventitious property, as is the case, for instance, with saying that it is white; since both one and existence refer, according to him, to an accident supervening on the object."[8] It follows, therefore, that existence is constituted through an accident, which then must be constituted by another accident and so on *ad infinitum,* which is absurd. He also criticizes Avicenna in the same passage for confusing the term existence with the true and inferring from this that, since the latter is an accident, the former is an accident too, which is a *non sequitur.*

More scathing, perhaps, is Averroes' critique of Avicenna's division of existing entities into possible absolutely, possible in themselves but necessary through another and finally necessary in themselves, as the title of one of his polemical tracts has it. In this lost tract, Averroes has no doubt argued, as he has done in his extant treatises, that the contention that an entity in particular, or the world in general, could be described as both possible and necessary at the same time is self-contradictory. For a thing cannot be both possible in itself and necessary through another, "unless its nature has been thoroughly altered."[9] Nor is it self-evident that the world is contingent, as Avicenna held in his attempt to formulate his classic argument for the existence of the Necessary Being, but rather the contrary. For once we posit the series of efficient causes, whether natural or intelligible, which determine the manner in which a given entity comes to be, then everything in the world, as well as the world itself, would become necessary, rather than possible or contingent. Moreover, to repudiate the necessity which determines the properties, modalities and powers of existing entities is to repudiate the wisdom of their Wise Creator, in the manner of atheists and materialists. It follows, as he puts it, "that in general, if we repudiate the existence of (necessary) causes and

8. *Tafsīr* III, p. 1279.
9. *Ibid.,* p. 1632.

effects, we would have no means of responding to the advocates of chance; I mean, those who assert that there is no Creator and that whatever happens in this world is the product of material causes."[10]

Averroes further observes that Avicenna's claim that the world is both possible and eternal is self-contradictory, too. For, with respect to eternal entities, there is no possibility, as Aristotle holds. For what is eternally possible, according to him, is eternally necessary.[11]

The other subsidiary criticisms leveled at Avicenna may be briefly mentioned. In the first place, he rejects Avicenna's contention that the existence of matter is demonstrable in metaphysics, rather than in physics, which is concerned primarily with the study of material entities. He also rejects his claim that the existence of the material cause of the universe, or Prime Matter, as well as its First Mover, is demonstrable in metaphysics, rather than physics; since Aristotle has actually demonstrated, in Books VII and VIII of the *Physics*, the existence of the First Mover of the heavens, or *primum mobile*, as well as that of Prime Matter.

In the second place, Averroes criticizes Avicenna's introduction of the so-called estimative faculty (*al-Wāhimah*), as a distinct faculty whereby the animal instinctively seeks the pleasurable and shuns the painful; or that whereby the sheep apprehend, in Avicenna's famous example, that grass is desirable and the wolf is fearful. For Averroes, the explicit teaching of the ancient philosophers, by whom he meant the Peripatetics with Aristotle at their head, is that the faculty whereby the wolf is recognized by the sheep as an enemy and the lamb as a friend is really the imaginative faculty. In that case, Averroes appears to argue that the introduction of the estimative faculty is superfluous. Aristotle had, in fact, stated at the end of *De Anima* that the imaginative faculty has two divisions, the deliberative or calculative, and the sensitive or instinctive; the latter is common to all animals, the former is peculiar to mankind. He then raises the question of whether 'imperfect animals' have both imagination and desire, and answers it by stating that "clearly they have feelings of pleasure and pain, and if they have these they must have desire."[12] By introducing the

---

10. *Al-Kashf*, p. 200.
11. *Tahāfut al-Tahāfut*, p. 98. Cf. Aristotle, *Metaphysics.* XII, 1071b 20.
12. *De Anima* III, 433b 1 f.

estimative faculty, which was accepted in medieval psychology, such as St. Thomas Aquinas', as axiomatic, Avicenna may have sought to exploit the ambiguity in Aristotle's words and to overcome it by introducing a generic type of the animal imagination, which he labeled the estimative.

3

The Critique of Ash'arite Theology (*Kalām*)

The Ash'arite Onslaught on the Philosophers

Prior to the rise of Mu'tazilite theology (*kalām*) in the eighth century, the study of Greek philosophy was looked upon with suspicion, on the ground that it was either foreign or pernicious. Al-Kindī, the first Muslim philosopher, who was known for his Mu'tazilite sympathies, undertook in the ninth century to rebut the charges of the anti-philosophical party. His major argument is that it is the duty of the conscientious 'searcher' after truth to seek it from whatever source it emanates from, "even if it were to come from distant races and nations different from us." He even accuses the anti-philosophical party, by whom he probably meant the Hanbalites and other traditionalists, of graft and social ambition. For they assume the posture of genuine seekers of truth, he writes, "simply to defend the positions of pre-eminence in society, as a means of gaining ascendancy or trafficking in religion; whereas they are devoid of religion altogether."[1]

Al-Kindī saw no contradiction between Greek philosophy and Islam and accordingly pledged his whole-hearted support to the principal articles of Islamic doctrine, such as the creation of the world *ex nihilo* and in time, the veracity of prophetic revelation and the resurrection of the

---

1. *Fi'l-Falsafah al-Ūla*, p. 81. (*On First Philosophy*, English trans. Alfred Ivry, p. 58.)

body. These were some of the critical issues in theological and philosophical circles around which controversy had raged at the time, and will continue to rage for centuries to come.

Be this as it may, the Mu'tazilites had been from the start well-disposed to use the rational or dialectical methods of the philosophers; but before long they came into conflict with the traditionalists whose champion in the ninth century was Aḥmed Ibn Ḥanbal. This famous tradition-monger, whose *Musnad* is one of the six canonical collections of Hadith, rejected out of hand any of the dialectical methods of proof that the Mu'tazilites had authorized. Condemned to prison and subjected to various forms of humiliation, including whipping, in the course of al-Ma'mūn's imposition of the famous Miḥna or Inquisition in 827, Ibn Ḥanbal stuck adamantly to his position that the Qur'an is "God's eternal and uncreated Word," in defiance of the Mu'tazilite contrary thesis that the Qur'an is created. In legal and theological matters, Ibn Ḥanbal adhered to the principle that only decisions or opinions which can be supported by textual passages from the Qur'an or the Traditions of the Prophet are justified. Half a century later, a new theological movement, championed by an ex-Mu'tazilite, Abū'l-Ḥasan al-Ash'ari, attempted to mediate between the Mu'tazilites and the Ḥanbalites, but remained essentially sympathetic to Ḥanbalism. This movement continued to gain ground throughout the tenth and eleventh centuries, at the hands of some of the greatest theologians of Islam, such as al-Bāqillani, al-Baghdādi and al-Juwayni.

However, the greatest standard-bearer of the Ash'arite and anti-philosophical cause in the eleventh century was Abū Hāmid al-Ghazālī, disciple of al-Juwayni. After being schooled in philosophy and logic at the hands of that master, he took up the cudgels against the Muslim Neoplatonists in a great work of philosophical polemic, *Tahāfut al-Falāsifah* (*Incoherence of the Philosophers*). In this work, al-Ghazālī takes the philosophers to task on twenty scores or questions, sixteen metaphysical and four physical, which, according to him, are "in conflict with the fundamentals of religion," i.e. Islam. With respect to ethics, mathematics and logic, he takes a neutral position. For ethical maxims, according to him, derive ultimately from the teaching of the prophets, who are divinely inspired; whereas mathematics, which deals with discontinuous quantity, as in arithmetic, or continuous quantity, as in geometry, has no bearing on religion whatsoever. Logic, on the other hand, is simply 'an instrument of thought,' which we are fully prepared to use in our "disputation with them [i.e. the philosophers] in this book [i.e. the *Incoherence*] by recourse to their own language; I mean by using their own logical idioms," as he writes in the preface to the *Incoherence*. He expresses in the same context, however, the conviction that the philosophers have not lived up, in their metaphysical sciences, to the rules they laid down in logic.[2]

With these prefatory remarks, al-Ghazālī proceeds to list the seventeen questions on which the philosophers should be declared heretical (*tabdī*) and the three questions on which they should be declared infidels (*takīr*).

In his rebuttal, called *Tahāfut al-Tahāfut* (*Incoherence of the Incoherence*), Averroes discusses systematically each of these questions and highlights the manner in which the Muslim Neoplatonists, i.e. al-Fārābī and Avicenna, who were the targets of al-Ghazālī's onslaught, have either distorted or misunderstood the teaching of Aristotle, as we have seen in the previous chapter. He accuses al-Ghazālī and the Ash'arites, in the same context, of misunderstanding the genuine intent of Scripture (*shar'*). In some places, al-Ghazālī himself is accused of downright sophistry.

As given by al-Ghazālī in his *Incoherence*, the list of questions, around which the controversy turned, begins with the pre-eternity and the post-eternity of the universe. The divergences among the philosophers are then mentioned by al-Ghazālī, who states that most of them adhered to the eternity of the universe, with the exception of Plato, who believed the universe to have been created in time, and Galen who suspended judgment on this question. He then proceeds to criticize the arguments of the advocates of eternity, advancing a series of arguments in refutation of their view. He proposes, as an alternative to pre-eternity, the view that the world was created in time by an act of eternal willing on the part of God, bypassing thereby the objection of the Neoplatonists

2. *Tahāfut al-Falāsifah*, p. 16.

that creation in time would entail necessarily a change in the divine essence, which is absurd.

In rejecting the thesis of post-eternity, al-Ghazālī refers to the Neoplatonists' argument that the world, being eternally possible, must exist eternally; since its corruption or cessation would entail, in fact, its eternity. For, if it were to cease to exist, its cessation subsequent to its existence would be succeeded by an endless period of time or 'an after,' and this in fact is tantamount to post-eternity, according to him. He counters this argument by simply reasserting God's infinite power, whereby He is able to bring the world into being or cause it to cease to exist, as He pleases and whenever He pleases.

In the third and fourth questions, al-Ghazālī accuses the philosophers of 'dissimulation' when they speak of God as the Maker or Creator of the world, since an eternal universe which has existed always, according to him, does not need a Maker or Creator to bring it into being. Accordingly, the arguments of those philosophers purporting to prove the existence of God are entirely hypocritical, induced by a malicious desire to deceive their hearers, in short, a form of 'dissimulation' (*talbīs*), as he calls it.

A group of questions (six to nine) deal with the philosophers' theory of divine attributes. To begin with, al-Ghazālī argues, their view of the identity of essence and existence amounts to a negation of divine attributes altogether. In the second place, the view of some of them, especially Avicenna, that God's knowledge is limited to the apprehension of universals, the knowledge of particulars being time-circumscribed according to them, is a flagrant repudiation of God's all-embracing knowledge, for which the philosophers deserve to be branded infidels.

Question seventeen, which opens the physical part of the *Incoherence*, turns on the question of the necessary correlation of causes and effects. The concept of such necessary correlation, according to al-Ghazālī, stems from the observation of the habitual correlation of events, which are alleged to be causes, and those which are alleged to be effects. However, properly understood, observation proves at best that the so-called effect, as the so-called correlate of the so-called cause, occurs with it and not through it (*ma'ahu lā bihi*). Such correlation, in fact, is a matter of contiguity, rather than causality. For as David Hume (d. 1776) was to show centuries later, observation or sense-experience is not a sufficient warrant of necessary correlation, but simply of subjective conjunction, born of habit. If so, argues al-Ghazālī, it is not excluded that such conjunction could be broken by God Almighty, whenever He wishes, as actually happens in the phenomenon of miracles, with which all Muslims concur. Thus, fire brought into contact with a flammable object is seen, as a rule, to burn it; but God Almighty can cause it miraculously to cool its object, rather than burn it, as happened in the case of the prophet Abraham, mentioned in Qur'an 21:69.[3]

The last two questions of the *Incoherence* deal with the immortality of the soul, on the one hand, and the resurrection of the body, on the other. On the first score, al-Ghazālī reviews the proofs advanced by the philosophers in support of the immortality of the soul, but pronounces them inconclusive. He then proceeds to argue that Scripture (*shar'*) has affirmed in no uncertain terms that the soul survives the destruction of the body at death, as the philosophers actually concede, but is reunited to the same body or one similar to it on the Day of Resurrection – a thesis which the philosophers deny. In that otherworldly condition and in association with the risen body, the soul is able to partake of intellectual or spiritual pleasures, which the philosophers also concede, as well as certain bodily pleasures, which they deny. However, one may ask, he writes: "What is the objection to admitting the conjunction of both spiritual and bodily pleasures as well as the corresponding miseries, as God says in Qur'an 32:17: 'No soul knows what was laid up for them secretly [of joyful relief as a reward for what they used to do].'" It follows, he adds, "that the existence of those noble states does not entail the exclusion of other [opposite] states. Rather, the conjunction of the two is more appropriate and the promise more perfect and is possible. It should be believed on the authority of Scripture."[4]

Averroes' Response to al-Ghazālī

In his own *Incoherence of the Incoherence*, as already mentioned, Averroes undertakes a thorough and systematic refutation of al-Ghazālī's

3. *Ibid.*, p. 282.
4. *Ibid.*, p. 355.

arguments one by one. His primary aim both here and elsewhere is to defend Aristotle against the strictures of the Ash'arites, in general, and al-Ghazālī, in particular, on the one hand, and to correct the errors of his Muslim interpreters, especially al-Fārābī and Avicenna, on the other.

In the first place, Averroes is particularly scathing in his attack on the Ash'arite theologians who, in their obsession with the notion of God's absolute omnipotence, have reduced the created order to total impotence or passivity. Every occurrence in the universe, according to them, is the product of God's direct and miraculous intervention, and thus created entities, whether animate or inanimate, are incapable of any initiative, since they are devoid of any active powers of any kind.

In the second place, Averroes accuses the Muslim Neoplatonists targeted by al-Ghazālī, including al-Fārābī and Avicenna, as we have seen in the previous chapter, of having misunderstood or distorted the teaching of Aristotle. Properly understood, this teaching is found to be perfectly compatible with the Holy Law (*Sharī'a*). Misled by the Neoplatonists' misunderstandings and distortions, which Averroes attempts in the course of the debate to correct, the Ash'arites have been led to reject the philosophers' methods of logical discourse, known as deduction (*qiyās*). This rejection, according to Averroes, is entirely indefensible, since the Qur'an itself has called upon mankind in a series of verses, such as 2:29 and 7:14, to 'look into,' 'consider' or 'reflect' on the wonders of creation, as a means of arriving at the knowledge of God as Creator. That knowledge can only be arrived at by recourse to the demonstrative methods of the philosophers. In addition, the Qur'an has drawn a clear distinction between those verses which are ambiguous (*mutashabihāt*) and those which are precise or unambiguous (*muhkamāt*), in Sura 3, verses 5–7, which read; "It is He who has revealed to you the Book, with verses which are precise in meaning and which are the Mother of the Book, and others which are ambiguous." It then adds that: "No one knows its interpretation except God and those well-grounded in knowledge," according to Averroes' own reading of that Qur'anic passage. By those well-grounded in knowledge, Averroes is categorical that only the philosophers or 'people of demonstration,' as he calls them, are intended. For they alone are able to undertake the interpretation of ambiguous passages in a conclusive way, by recourse to the highest method of proof, known as the demonstrative. The Mutakallimun are at best able to use the inferior, dialectical method, and the masses at large, the lowest, rhetorical method.

The key to fathoming the depth of the controversy which set the Ash'arites at loggerheads with the philosophers is the proper application of the sound methods of interpretation to the issues, which, according to al-Ghazālī, divided them. The three principal issues on which the philosophers are charged with irreligion (*kufr*) are found on close scrutiny to rest on a misunderstanding or misinterpretation of the Qur'anic texts in question. Take as an example the first of these, the eternity of the world. Carefully considered, the differences between the philosophers and the Mutakallimun are not so vast as to justify the above charge of irreligion. They are reducible, in fact, to purely semantic or verbal divergences only. For, of the three varieties of entities, argues Averroes, namely, God, particular entities and the world as a whole, both parties are in agreement on the status of the first two, but disagree on the status of the third or its duration, which is infinite *a parte ante* and *a parte post* according to the philosophers, but finite according to the Mutakallimun. However, the philosophers do not regard the world, which has existed since all time, as 'really eternal', which is synonymous with uncaused, nor really created in time (*ḥādith*), which is absurd.[5]

In rebutting the thesis of 'eternal will,' proposed by al-Ghazālī and the Ash'arites as a way out of the dilemma that creating the world in time entails necessarily a change in God's essence, His will or its relation to the world, Averroes begins by drawing attention to the difference between the two concepts of will and action (*fi'l*), as predicated of God. To suppose that the world, willed by God eternally, has come into being after a certain lapse of time is logically admissible, but not that it has followed His *action* after such a lapse of time, unless we assume that He was impeded by some defect or impotence, which is absurd.[6] In other words, the world is to be viewed as the product of God's action, not His will, and no interval can be conceived between His action and the product of that action; i.e. the world.

5. *Faṣl al-Maqāl*, p. 42.
6. *Tahāfut al-Tahāfut*, pp. 36 and 9 f.

Moreover, the nature of will consists in being a power to do one of two contrary alternatives. Thus to posit an eternal will contradicts the very nature of will. Add to this that will signifies a desire on the part of the agent to do a certain action, which once it is done the desire ceases and this means, once more, that the concept of an eternal will is self-contradictory. Accordingly, 'demonstration' compels us to concede, Averroes concludes, that neither of the two modes of action, by will or by nature, is really applicable to God, who is spoken of in Scripture (*shar'*) as a willing Agent metaphorically.[7] Natural willing is excluded on the ground that it subjects God to a state of compulsion, and free will is excluded on the ground that it presupposes some want or other and is a form of affection (*infi'āl*) or change, of which God is free. Nonetheless, Averroes does not deny that God may be spoken of as a free and willing agent, provided it is understood that His will, like His knowledge, is entirely different from human knowledge and that the modality (*kayfiyah*) of these two attributes, as predicated of God, is unknowable.[8]

Moreover, contrary to al-Ghazālī's charge that the philosophers' thesis of a universe existing since all time is contrary to the teaching of Scripture (*shar'*), a careful reading of Qur'anic texts pertaining to the origination of the world would reveal that the 'explicit' intent of many such verses is that the 'form' of the universe is created in time (*muḥdath*), whereas its existence itself and its duration are continuous *a parte ante* and *a parte post.* Thus verse 11:9, which states that it is "He who created the heavens and the earth in six days, while His throne rested upon water," implies on the surface of it that the water, the throne and their temporal duration are all eternal. Similarly, verse 41:10, which states: "Then He arose to heaven, while it was smoke," implies that the heavens were created from something already existing, which is smoke.[9]

Be this as it may, Averroes goes on to argue, the Mutakallimun, whether they admit it or not, base their thesis that the world is created *ex nihilo* and in time, not on the explicit statements of Scripture, but rather on their own arbitrary interpretations of those statements. For if we scour

7. *Ibid.*, pp. 9 f.
8. *Ibid.*, p. 149.
9. *Ibid.*, p. 43.

the Qur'an thoroughly, we will not find a single text asserting that God first existed with pure not-being ('*adam*), then He existed with the world which did not exist before. Accordingly, the claim of the Mutakallimun that the creation of the world in time is explicitly stated in the Qur'an, or has been consecrated by the consensus (*ijmā'*) of the community, is entirely gratuitous. Contrariwise, they are, like the philosophers, adepts of interpretation, which is an obligation incumbent on the learned, who even if they are in error, are deserving of pardon. The Prophet himself has said, Averroes continues: "If a judge uses his discretion (*ijtihād*) and is right, he deserves two rewards; whereas, if he is mistaken, he deserves one reward only." "What judge is greater," Averroes then asks, "than he who judges that existing things are such or not such?"[10] By the latter judge(s) Averroes clearly meant the philosophers or the learned in general, who have been charged by Scripture itself to investigate, consider or reflect on the wonders of creation, as already mentioned.

The responsibility for interpreting the 'ambiguous' passages of Scripture is not, then, universal or open-ended, according to Averroes. Drawing on Aristotle's division of arguments or modes of discourse, in *Sophistica* and *Rhetorica*, into demonstrative, dialectical and rhetorical, he proceeds to divide mankind into three distinct groups, the demonstrative, by whom he means the philosophers, the dialectical, by whom he means the theologians and the rhetorical, by whom he means the masses at large.[11] Those three groups or classes differ radically in their ability to reason, as well as in the degree of 'assent' (*tasdīq*) they are able to achieve when it comes to interpreting the ambiguous passages of Scripture.

On the second major question of God's knowledge, Averroes faults Avicenna for regarding that knowledge as universal, but rejects al-Ghazālī's charge that the philosophers have stripped God of knowledge altogether and reduced Him thereby to the status of the dead; since it is axiomatic, according to them, that knowledge is a corollary of life. The Ash'arites in general and al-Ghazālī in particular could be said to be guilty here of what may be called the fallacy of predication. In predicating knowledge of God, he argues, it is equally wrong to describe this

10. *Ibid.*, p. 43.
11. *Ibid.*, p. 426.

knowledge, either as universal or particular, by analogy to human knowledge. For the two modes of knowledge, the divine and the human, are radically different, human knowledge being the *effect* of the thing known, whereas divine knowledge is the *cause* of the thing known, and therefore cannot be described as either universal or particular.[12] In the *Incoherence*, Averroes goes so far as to assert that the mode of God's knowledge, as well as that of His will, is entirely unknown to us.[13]

Notwithstanding, in the *Large Commentary on the Metaphysics*, Averroes dwells at length on God's knowledge of existing entities, rejecting, on the one hand, the view of Themistius that God apprehends the multitude of existing entities making up the universe at once, and that of Avicenna, that He apprehends them by a universal mode of apprehension, which is not liable to change, on the other. Both views, according to Averroes, do not accord with the teaching of Aristotle, which he interprets to mean that God, or the First Principle, "In so far as He knows himself only, knows all existing entities through that existence of which He is the cause." Thus the term knowledge is predicated of God's knowledge and our own equivocally. For His knowledge, he concludes, "is the cause of the existing entity, whereas the existing entity is the cause of our knowledge, and therefore cannot be described either as universal or particular."[14] The specific reason he gives in this context is that, in so far as particulars exist in potentiality, or rather in so far as their essence is potential, the knowledge of such particulars is purely potential; but clearly such knowledge is unworthy of God, in whom there is no element of potentiality whatsoever. Moreover, particulars being infinite in number, it is obvious that they cannot be encompassed by any mode of knowledge, and this would amount to stripping God of the all-embracing knowledge proper to Him. In short, God's knowledge should be regarded as entirely *sui generis*, and its mode, as was said earlier, is unknowable to us.

Perhaps the most original part of Averroes' view of the mode of God's knowledge is the assertion that God's knowledge of particulars is the corollary of His knowledge of Himself, which he ascribes to Aristotle.

12. *Ibid.*, p. 468.
13. *Ibid.*, p. 149.
14. *Tafsīr* III, pp. 1707 f.

Aristotle, it will be recalled, had in *Metaphysics* XII, 1074b20 f., reduced God's knowledge exclusively to self-knowledge, arguing that He can only think "of what is most divine and precious," i. e. Himself. For, as he goes on to ask rhetorically: "Are there not some things about which it is incredible that it [God] should think?", adding with a melancholy sense of despair, in his effort to spare God the indignity of idle curiosity, so to speak, "For there are even some things which it is better not to see than to see." Aristotle's commentators have, therefore, struggled valiantly with the question of God's knowledge, in an attempt to circumvent the obvious objections to this narcissistic mode of divine knowledge, which is clearly inadequate. As Sir W. D. Ross (d. 1971), one of the greatest Aristotelian scholars of our time, has put it: "God, as conceived by Aristotle, has a knowledge which is not a knowledge of the universe, and an influence on the universe which does not flow from His knowledge."[15] Averroes was the first leading Aristotelian to come up with this original interpretation; namely, that in knowing Himself as the cause of the universe, God knows at the same time the totality of effects which flow from Him as their cause. This interpretation did not only overcome the inadequacy inherent in the Aristotelian notion of divine knowledge, it also became the generally accepted interpretation in Medieval Scholastic circles. Thus St. Thomas Aquinas (d. 1274), the other great Aristotelian of the post-Averroist era, states explicitly in his commentary on *Metaphysics* XII, lectio XI: "Quod igitur a prima principio, quod est Deus, dependeat coelum et tota natura, ut dictum est, patet quod Deus cognoscendo Seipsum, omnia cognoscit;" that is, "in so far as heaven and the whole of nature depend on the First Principle, who is God, as is stated [by Aristotle], it is clear that in knowing Himself, God knows all things."

The third question on which al-Ghazālī accuses the philosophers of irreligion is that of resurrection. The arguments of the philosophers in support of the immortality of the soul, he contends, to begin with, are inconclusive, in so far as they are predicated on its simplicity and immateriality, which, according to him, they have not demonstrated in a satisfactory way. Now, if the arguments of the philosophers are of no avail

15. Ross, *Aristotle*, p. 183.

when it comes to the critical issue of the soul's immortality, the only recourse left them is Scripture, which asserts unequivocally the resurrection of the soul in conjunction with the body in the after-life, wherein it will partake of the spiritual and bodily pleasures vouchsafed to the pious as set down in explicit terms in the Qur'an.[16]

Resurrection and the Concurrence of Philosophy and Religion

In his rebuttal, Averroes concedes that survival after death (*ma'ād*), as he prefers to call it, is a matter "regarding which religious laws (*sharā'i'*) and the demonstrations of the philosophers are in accord."[17] In fact, religion and philosophy, he explains, do not differ regarding the *reality* of this survival, but only its *mode*, namely, whether it is spiritual or corporeal. They do differ, however, regarding the kind of representations of this mode given in Scripture, as well as the pleasures attendant upon it. Some Scriptures, by which he probably meant the Christian, dwell on 'spiritual or angelic' pleasures, whereas other Scriptures, meaning the Qur'an, dwell on 'sensuous representations,' which are more effective, he says, than spiritual representations "in moving the souls of the general public."[18]

Averroes then goes on to explain the reason for the concurrence of both philosophy and religion, regarding survival after death. This survival, or rather the expectation of it, he argues, is one of the pillars of religious laws, which "tend towards the management of human affairs, upon which the very existence of man, qua man, and his attainment of that happiness proper to him actually depend."[19] Moreover, the religious laws are the cornerstones of both theoretical and practical virtues, as well as the practical arts which are essential for man's survival in this world. Although he is categorical that both the theoretical and the practical virtues are the preconditions of man's happiness in this world and the world to come, he explains that the practical or moral virtues are primary, especially since they cannot become ingrained in the soul "without the knowledge of God Almighty and glorifying Him by those forms of worship, laid down in a

---

16. *Tahāfut al-Falāsifah*, pp. 354 f.
17. *Al-Kashf*, p. 240; cf. *Tahāfut al-Tahāfut*, pp. 282 f.
18. *Al-Kashf*, pp. 242 f.
19. *Tahāfut*, p. 581.

given religion, such as offerings, prayers, petitions and such like."[20] The philosophers believe, he adds, that 'the general principles' of religious laws should not be questioned or scrutinized, by asking such questions as whether God should be worshiped or not, whether He exists or not and whether happiness in the hereafter is true or not. The reason he gives is symptomatic of this major practical or pragmatic concession he is willing to make, with respect to religious beliefs or practices. It consists in the fact that all religious laws, as we have seen, concur in the reality of an otherworldly existence, although they differ with respect to its modality, just as they concur in acknowledging the existence of the Maker (*Sāni'*), His attributes and His actions. The chief merit of religion, as compared with philosophy, is that it addresses all classes of men and defines the actions which conduce to their happiness in the hereafter, unlike philosophy which addresses a small group of men and defines the conditions of "their intellectual happiness."[21]

If one were to ask whether any religion is superior to any other, Averroes' answer appears to be that the philosopher, and by extension any intelligent searcher after truth, is duty-bound to choose "the best [religion] in his age, although all of them are equally true."[22] For none of them is superior to the rest except to the extent that the laws and precepts it lays down are superior to those laid down by others. For that religion (by which he meant Islam), by stipulating the performance of ritual prayers at fixed times and in a specific manner, is found to have contributed to the life of virtue to a higher degree than any other religion. A mark of the best religion, in fact, is that it abrogates its predecessors, as Christianity did abrogate Judaism and Islam abrogated both in due course.[23]

Another instance of the superiority of Islam to other religions is then given by Averroes. If we consider the account of resurrection and the life after death given in the Qur'an, we will find that the graphic, sensuous representations of the pleasures and tribulations which the pious or

20. *Ibid.*, p. 581.
21. *Ibid.*, p. 582.
22. *Ibid.*, p. 583.
23. *Ibid.*, p. 583.

wicked are accorded are more conducive to compelling adherence to a life of virtue than the spiritual representations given in the Scriptures of other religions, meaning no doubt Christianity.[24]

The remaining seventeen questions of al-Ghazālī's *Incoherence of the Philosophers* are explicitly stated by him to justify the lesser charge of heresy or innovation (*tabdī'*), rather than the more serious charge of irreligion (*takfīr*). They consist primarily of a series of accusations leveled at the philosophers for their failure to make good their claims to prove convincingly that God exists as the Creator of the world, His unity, His simplicity, His incorporeity and His knowledge of Himself, let alone His knowledge of particulars. Nor are they more successful in their attempt to prove that the soul, as they claim, is a self-subsistent and indestructible entity, as we have seen earlier. Finally, their cosmological thesis that the heavenly spheres are animate and move in circles at the behest of God, and are in addition conversant with all particular occurrences in the lower or sublunary world, as they call it, are entirely groundless.

Averroes counters these accusations by observing, as we have seen in the previous chapter, that those charges may be justified where the views of al-Fārābī, Avicenna and the Neoplatonists in general are concerned, but not where the teaching of Aristotle properly interpreted is concerned. A tacit assumption, as we have also seen, is that those Neoplatonists have either misunderstood or distorted the teaching of the Master.

Causality Revindicated

Perhaps the most significant of the above-mentioned seventeen questions is the one in which al-Ghazālī launches a sustained attack on the Aristotelian concept of causality, to which we have already referred. The crux of the argument is that the Aristotelian concept of necessary causal correlation between natural occurrences is not tenable and rests exclusively on the evidence of the senses or observation. It is far more reasonable and consistent with Islamic doctrine to refer all natural occurrences to the direct intervention of God, the Sole Agent in the world, who acts miraculously whenever He pleases, interrupting thereby

24. *Ibid.*, p. 585.

the habitual course of events, described as causal correlation by the philosophers.

In his rebuttal, Averroes begins by asserting that "the repudiation of efficient causes observed in objects of sense is a form of sophistry, wherein the speaker either denies by his tongue what is in his heart, or is the victim of a sophistical doubt."[25] For no one can reasonably deny that every action or occurrence has an underlying cause, whether natural or supernatural. Whenever the cause of such an action or occurrence is unknown or undetermined, it is deemed to be unknown. For in the last analysis, as Aristotle has affirmed in *Analytica Posteriora* I, 71b10 f. and elsewhere, the knowledge of the fact is tantamount to the knowledge of the cause on which that fact actually depends. It follows that the repudiation of causality is tantamount to the repudiation of knowledge altogether, and with it what may be called the whole scientific enterprise, as sceptics and agnostics have always done.

A further argument of Averroes in rebuttal of al-Ghazālī's repudiation of necessary causal correlation consists in showing that it is inimical to any rational view of the universe. For it is self-evident, he argues, that existing things possess certain natures or properties, which determine the kinds of actions associated with them and even the definitions appropriate to them. "Hence, if an existing entity did not have a nature proper to it, it would not have a name or definition proper to it; then all things would be reducible to one thing and not one thing at the same time."[26] For in the case of every such entity, we are justified in asking whether it has an action or passion proper to it or not; otherwise "the one will not be one, and once the nature of the one is removed, the nature of being is removed . . . and then nothingness will ensue necessarily."[27] In other words, we will be left with nothing, as the nihilists contend.

Averroes then goes on to reaffirm Aristotle's thesis that a complete explanation of a given entity or occurrence is not possible except in terms of the four causes, the material, the formal, the efficient and the final. The Mutakallimun themselves, he adds, concede that there are certain

25. *Ibid.*, p. 519.
26. *Ibid.*, p. 520.
27. *Ibid.*, p. 521.

conditions which are necessary concomitants of the conditioned, such as life, which is a necessary condition of knowledge, and knowledge, which is a necessary condition of will. They are also willing to draw the kind of necessary inference from the nature of a given entity, such as the perfection of an artifact, being indicative of the rationality of the artisan. Now, "reason is nothing more than the apprehension of existing things by means of their causes; so that whoever repudiates causes actually repudiates reason."[28] In these circumstances, we would be forced to deny, in the manner of the ancient Sophists, that any kind of genuine knowledge is possible and that, by contrast, all is pure conjecture. However, Averroes writes, paraphrasing Aristotle's famous response to the Sophists: "Whoever asserts that there is not a single kind of knowledge which is necessary will be forced to admit that this assertion of his is not necessary.[29]

Averroes turns next to al-Ghazālī's contention that the correlation between causes and effects is simply a matter of habit, born of the repeated observation of correlated events, as David Hume was later to argue. Then he asks, "What do the Mutakallimun mean by habit? Is it the habit of God as the agent in question; that of existing entities or our own habit in judging the observed occurrence or series of occurrences?" The first alternative, he asserts, is false, because God's ways, as the Qur'an (35: 41) has put it, are unalterable, which is the reverse of habitual. The second alternative is also false, because habit is predicable of animate entities only; if predicated of inanimate entities, habit becomes a synonym of nature. The third alternative entails that "habit is nothing more than the action of reason, as determined by its very nature whereby it is actually designated as reason."[30] Now, reason, as stated above, is the faculty which apprehends entities or events as possessing certain determinate natures and are known only once their causes are known or determined.

In his *Exposition of the Methods of Proof* (*al-Kashf*), Averroes pursues the discussion of the question of causation further against the backdrop of the Ash'arite notion of contingency, expounded by a leading Ash'arite theologian, al-Juwayni, also known as Abū' l-Ma'āli (d. 1086), teacher of

28. *Ibid.*, p. 522.
29. *Ibid.*, p. 522.
30. *Ibid.*, p. 523.

al-Ghazālī himself, in his treatise, *al-Niẓāmiyah*. In this treatise, this theologian argues, in a manner reminiscent of Avicenna, that everything in the world is contingent or possible in the sense that it could have been otherwise. What determines its existence in the specific way it actually exists is the divine will, which could have determined that it should be otherwise.

For Averroes, the falsity of this position is self-evident and is contradicted by the fact that an entity, such as man, is constituted in a determinate way and no other, and a westward or eastward motion is determined by a hidden cause which may be unknown to us. In neither case are we justified in speaking of contingency, which is symptomatic of ignorance. It is like a person who is not proficient in a certain art regarding the features of a given artifact as contingent, in the sense that they could be otherwise; whereas a skilled artisan would hold, contrariwise, that every aspect of that artifact is necessary, and is in that respect the work of a skilled artisan.

In the same way, created entities may be compared to works of art, which manifest the skill and wisdom of their Creator. Now, wisdom is the knowledge, to the highest degree, of the causes which have gone into the making of a given entity. Thus, if things did not have any necessary causes determining their existence in the way they have come to exist, then there would be no wisdom in their existing in the way they exist. To deny the specific properties or natures pertaining to created entities and to regard them as contingent is to deny the wisdom of the Creator and to relinquish the whole creation to the vagaries of chance (*ittifāq*). In addition, we would have no means of demonstrating the existence of the Creator, whose wise workmanship is manifested in His rationally ordered creation. To resort to those proofs of God's existence which rest on temporality (*ḥudūth*), as the Mutakallimun in general have done, or contingency, as Avicenna and al-Juwayni have done, is of no avail; because they rest on premises which are questionable. Thus, the Ash'arites, who favor the first argument, base it on the premise that the world is temporal, which they base in turn on the proposition that the world is made up of indivisible particles or atoms, which are temporal or ephemeral, like the world in its totality. However, if we probe this argument carefully, we will find that the atomic theory upon which it rests is intractable, not only as far as the general public is concerned, but even as regards skilled logicians. The same is true of their proposition that the world is temporal or created in time (*muḥdath*), since the question can be raised with respect to its creator in time (*muḥdith*): is he temporal or eternal? This question is equally intractable and the argument which rests upon it is intractable, too.[31]

As for the argument from contingency, it is purely gratuitous, as we have seen, since the proposition that the world is contingent is rooted in our ignorance of the causes which determine the natures of existing entities, and contradicts the wisdom of the Creator who has ordered the world rationally.

Averroes' Own Proofs of the Existence of God

As an alternative, Averroes proposes two other proofs for the existence of God, "to which the Precious Book, [i.e. the Qur'an] has drawn attention," that of providence (*'ināyah*) and that of invention (*ikhtirā'*). The first rests on the double premise that everything in the world exists in order to serve the well-being of mankind, and as such is the product of the action of a willful Agent, or God. This is confirmed, according to Averroes, by the way in which the sun and the moon, the four seasons, the rivers and the seas are found to contribute to that well-being.[32]

The second proof rests on two premises, the first of which is that the great multitude of plants, animals and heavenly bodies are all the product of invention. This is a self-evident proposition and is borne out by the observation of the emergence of life in animate objects and the ceaseless motions of the heavenly bodies, which are commanded to 'subserve us,' and is confirmed by the Qur'an (verse 22:72), which states that "those whom you call upon, besides God, will never create a fly, even if they band together." Now it is obvious that what is invented must have an inventor, and this is the second premise of this proof.

It follows, he goes on to argue, that for one to know God, one must know the essences of things, so as to be able to discern the underlying

31. Al-Kashf, p. 136.
32. *Ibid.*, pp. 150 and 194 f.

inventive power which has brought them into existence. This is also confirmed by the Qur'anic verse 7:184, which states: "Have they not considered the kingdom of the heavens and the earth and whatever God has created?" Moreover, whoever probes the meaning of wisdom underlying the existence of any given entity, I mean, he writes, "the reason for which it was created and the purpose intended thereby will gain a fuller understanding of the proof of providence",[33] and by extension, although Averroes does not mention it specifically, that of invention, as well. In the sequel, he proceeds to list the Qur'anic verses purporting to support both proofs, either singly or in conjunction. He concludes that the chief merit of those two proofs is that they are addressed to both the learned and the public at large; the only difference between the two groups being that the latter are content with the evidence of the senses, whereas the former are able to supplement that evidence with rational demonstrations.

---

33. *Ibid.*, p. 151.

4

Logic and Theory of Knowledge

Logic in Relation to the Other Sciences

In late antiquity, logic, embodied chiefly in Aristotle's logical corpus, was referred to as the *Orpanon*, meaning tool or instrument. The same term, or rather its Arabic equivalent, was applied to Aristotelian logic in the Arab–Islamic tradition, even by anti-philosophical authors, such as al-Ghazālī; he refers to logic as the instrument of thought (*ālat al-nazar*) and regards it as perfectly innocuous from a religious point of view, as we have seen in an earlier chapter.

Today Aristotelian or traditional logic is referred to as 'formal logic,' to distinguish it from mathematical or symbolic logic, and is believed to serve as a prelude, or as Kant calls it, a propaedeutic, to the study of the other philosophical sciences.

Averroes concurs fully with the last sentiment, as appears from his statement in the preface to his *Paraphrase of the Physics*, where he writes:

"It is clear that whoever wishes to study this book, should start first by studying the art of logic, either in Abū Naṣr (al-Fārābī's) book or more briefly in the small epitome, which we have written."[1] Although Aristotle does not make this claim explicitly in the *Physics* or any of the substantive

---

1. Jawāmiʿ al-Samaʿ al-Tabiʿi, in *Rasāʾil Ibn Rushd*, p. 8.

treatises, as far as I know, it appears to have been part of the Islamic philosophical tradition, best illustrated in the parallel assertion of Averroes' predecessor, Avempace, in the preface to his own *Paraphrase of the Physics*.

Averroes proceeds next to argue that logic is indispensable for clearly distinguishing the 'scientific' from the 'dialectical' statements made in the *Physics*, as well as the other Aristotelian treatises. It was part of Aristotle's practice, as every one of his readers will at once note, to start the discussion of these subjects with a review of the views of his predecessors, before proceeding to an exposition of his own views. The former were clearly the 'dialectical' or weak views, to which Averroes is alluding here.

As far as his own logical writings are concerned, we might mention that Averroes is known to have written commentaries on, or paraphrases of, the whole Aristotelian logical corpus, as well as the *Rhetoric* and the *Poetics*, which formed part of that corpus in the Arab and Syriac traditions. In addition, he has written a commentary on Porphyry's *Isagoge* or *Introduction to Logic*, which played a decisive role in the development of logic, both in the Arabic–Muslim and the Latin–Medieval worlds. We might begin with his summary or paraphrase of the *Categories*, which in fact formed the first part of the *Organon*. Here Averroes states that his aim in this work is to summarize Aristotle's intentions in the *Categories*, which he divides into three parts: 1) a prefatory part in which Aristotle lays down the rules of definition, on which the book is supposed to turn; and 2) a part in which he lists the ten categories, one by one, gives a description (*rasm*) of each, then divides them into their generally accepted kinds and gives their general properties; 3) in the third part, he deals with the general categories, or most of them.

In the exposition that follows, Averroes defines equivocal, derivative and univocal terms in a manner which corresponds roughly to Aristotle's account in *Categories* Ia1–5. He then divides the categories into four classes. The first class consists of those which are predicable of a subject, but are not present in a subject, such as man and animal, which are indicative of the essence of the *definiendum*. These are the specific or generic attributes. The second class consists of those which are present in a subject, but are not predicable of a subject, by which Averroes means accidental attributes, such as whiteness or blackness. The third class consists of those attributes which are predicable of a subject and are present in a subject, by which he means essential attributes, such as knowledge which is predicable of the knower, or writing which is also predicable of the knower, but in two different respects. For knowledge belongs to the knower essentially, unlike writing, which may belong to him accidentally. The fourth class consists of those categories which are neither predicable of a subject nor present in a subject, by which Aristotle means substance, as defined in *Categories* 5. This substance both Aristotle and Averroes identify with the individual, such as Zayd and 'Amr in Averroes' examples. The difference between substance and accident, whether general or particular, is that substance is, by definition, that which is never present in a subject nor predicable of a subject, since it is the subject of which all accidents and attributes are predicated. Accidents, on the other hand, belong, by definition, to the class of the predicables.

The categories are then given, along Aristotelian lines, as ten: Substance (*jawhar*), quantity, quality, relation, place, time, state, possession, action and passion. In his discussion of substance, Averroes distinguishes, like Aristotle, between primary and secondary substance. The former is identified with the individual, as already mentioned, secondary substance with the species, to which individuals belong as parts to the whole. Species itself is part of genus, both of which are instances of secondary substance.

A characteristic feature of secondary substances is that their names or definitions are predicable of the subject, contrary to primary substance, which, as already mentioned, is neither predicable of a subject nor present in a subject. Another unique characteristic of substance is that it admits of no contraries and is not susceptible of receiving opposites.[2]

After discussing the categories of quality, quantity, relation, action, passion and state, Averroes turns to the discussion of correlative terms and contraries, along essentially Aristotelian lines, and concludes with the discussion of motion, which is the central theme of the *Physics*. This is another instance of the correlation of the sciences of logic and physics. He lists here

---

2. Cf. *Talkhīs Kitāb al-Maqūlat*, in Jihami, *Talkhīs Mantiq Aristu* I, p. 24.

six categories of motion; generation and its opposite, which is corruption; growth, whose opposite is diminution, alteration or change of quality; and finally motion in place (locomotion) or rest. He concludes that all forms of motion or change may be described as alteration, except locomotion.[3]

It is well-known that the core of Aristotelian logic is the theory of the syllogism, embodied in the *Analytica Posteriora*, called in the Arabic sources the *Book of Demonstration* (*Kitāb al-Burhān*). After discussing propositions in the *Book of Interpretation* (*al-'Ibārah*), Averroes opens the discussion with a division of propositions into absolute or existing in fact (i.e. actual), necessary and possible. That is why, he says, the parts of the syllogism are divided according to the mood of the premises, which are either affirmative or negative, universal or particular and finally indefinite. He then discusses the conversion of propositions and the rules of such conversion, followed by a discussion of the three figures of the syllogism, to which a fourth figure was later added by Galen. He observes in this context that the fourth figure is unnatural, since in logic we are really concerned with that syllogism which the mind arrives at naturally by reference to the desired conclusion. The fourth figure "was overlooked by Aristotle, because it does not conform to reality and is almost indefinite,"[4] as he writes.

Demonstration and Scientific Knowledge

In the summary of the *Analytica Posteriora*, Averroes begins by paraphrasing Aristotle's dictum that all instruction and 'intellectual learning' is rooted in pre-existing knowledge, which is shown to be evident by induction (*istiqrā'*). Like Aristotle, he then instances reasoning in mathematics and other theoretical sciences to illustrate this point. Even inferior forms of reasoning, such as the dialectical and rhetorical, rest on pre-existing knowledge of particulars, unlike the former which rests on self-evident premises which are universal in character.

Pre-existing knowledge is then divided into knowledge of the fact that the thing exists, which he identifies with assent (*tasdīq*) and the meaning of

3. *Ibid.*, p. 73.
4. *Ibid.*, pp. 172 f.

the term used, which he identifies with conception (*taṣawwur*). These two divisions were at the basis of the Arabic logical tradition and have been part of the legacy of Stoic logic. This pre-existing knowledge, he adds, is not a matter of recalling a particular, previously perceived, or else it would be tantamount to recollection, as Plato held; and although sensation enters into it, it is really intuitive, as when we recognize, upon perceiving a particular figure, that it is actually a triangle.

Next, Averroes reiterates a fundamental tenet of Aristotle's theory of knowledge, according to which genuine or scientific knowledge does not consist, as the Sophists held, in the apprehension of an accidental aspect of the thing known, but rather in the apprehension of the cause of the object known and the fact that without that cause that object could not have come to exist in the way it is. Such knowledge can only be attained through demonstration, as conjoined to definition, on which the second part of *Analytica Posteriora* actually turns.[5]

Demonstration is then defined as a type of "deduction (*qiyās*) which imparts the knowledge of the thing as it actually is, through the cause whereby it is what it is." To meet this condition, the premises of such demonstrative knowledge must be true, primary and immediate; that is, not known through a middle term. They must also be better known than the conclusion.

That the premise of a demonstration must be true implies: 1) that false premises are misleading because they give the impression that the thing which does not exist actually exists; 2) that they are immediate, or not involving a middle term, which implies that they do not need a demonstration; 3) that they are the causes of the thing known, which implies, as already mentioned, that a thing is known when its cause is known; 4) that they are primary, which implies that they are prior to the conclusion; 5) that they are better known than the conclusion, which implies that they are better known in terms of the name denoting the object or the fact that it actually exists. He then defines the two senses of better known; namely, for us, which refers to compound and perceptual knowledge; or by nature, which refers to the knowledge of the simple

5. Cf. *Kitāb al-Burhan*, in Jihami, *Talkhīs Mantiq Aristu* II, p. 373.

elements from which compound statements are made and which is, for that reason, farthest removed from sense-perception. By farthest removed from sense-perception should be understood universal, as against particulars which are nearest to us.[6]

The first principles of demonstration or premises are: a) either such that they cannot be demonstrated and are not self-evident, in which case they are called postulates; or b) are self-evident, in which case they are called generally accepted principles.

Those who deny that demonstration is productive of certain or scientific knowledge include: 1) those who hold that the premises of demonstration require a demonstration, which in turn requires a demonstration and so on *ad infinitum*; this will render demonstration impossible; or 2) those who hold that everything requires a demonstration in a circular, not a rectilinear way. This happens in the fallacy known as petition of principle or vicious circle. Averroes refutes the two arguments by reasserting that not everything is known through demonstration, for as we have seen, demonstration ultimately rests on self-evident principles or premises which are not known through demonstration, but rather intuitively or immediately. Thus both the infinite regress and the vicious circle are thereby averted.

Next, Averroes argues, in strict Aristotelian fashion, that there are two types of demonstration used in scientific discourse, the one which demonstrates the fact, or that the thing is (*anna*) and that which demonstrates the reason of the fact (*lima*), or *oti* and *dioti*, as Aristotle has put it. The difference between the two, he goes on to explain, is that the first type, which imparts the knowledge of the fact that the thing exists, rests on mediate premises, whose causes are remote. By contrast, the second type, which imparts the knowledge of the reason of the fact, rests on premises whose causes are proximate and immediate. Thus we may infer the proximity of the planets from the fact that they do not twinkle, and the reason why they do not twinkle from the fact that they are proximate. Moreover, knowledge of the fact does not constitute genuine or scientific knowledge, unless it is conjoined to the knowledge of the

6. *Ibid.*, p. 375. Cf. Aristotle, *Analytica Posteriora* I, 71b 26.

reason of the fact. Thus, by science we should understand a system of propositions, each of which flows from the original premises or first principles, according to the rules of deduction. Some sciences, such as physics, impart the knowledge of the fact, unlike mathematics, which by reason of the abstract principles it consists of, imparts the knowledge of the reason of the fact. "That is why," Averroes writes, "mathematicians are frequently unaware of the existence of the thing, but only of its cause; since they investigate things in so far as they are separate from matter, the existence of a thing being always in conjunction with matter."[7] In other words, mathematicians are concerned with abstract concepts or relations, unlike physicists who are concerned with existing material entities.

The second part of *Analytica Posteriora*, as already mentioned, deals with definition, which is the subject of conception (*taṣawwur*), as against demonstration, which is the subject of assent (*taṣdīq*) or judgment. The most general differences between the two are then given as follows: 1) Definition yields the essence of the *definiendum*, whereas demonstration yields what is extraneous to the essence; namely, its essential attributes or relations. 2) Demonstrations, on the other hand, are constructed by means of differentiation. Thus we define a man as a walking, two-footed, upright animal to distinguish him from animals which do not possess those attributes. It is for this reason that those attributes are called by the logicians differentiae (*fuṣūl*). When these differentiae are accidental rather than essential, the consequence is a description (*rasm*), rather than a definition (*ḥadd*). 3) Demonstrations may yield affirmative or negative conclusions, whereas definitions can only yield knowledge of the *definiendum* in an affirmative way. 4) Moreover, demonstration can yield knowledge of particulars, whereas definitions are always universal. 5) The first principles of demonstration are known through definition, but not vice versa. In fact, the first principles of demonstration, whether postulates or axioms, as we have seen, are definitions which are indemonstrable.

How definitions are formulated is then discussed. The first point Averroes makes is that it is impossible that they should be formulated by demonstration; for demonstration is a form of deduction or syllogism

---

7. *Kitāb al-Burhan*, in Jihāmi, *Talkhīs Mantiq Aristu* II, p. 409.

(*qiyās*), which requires a middle term; whereas definitions are formulated directly, without any intermediary. Moreover, as first principles of demonstration, definitions cannot be known through demonstration, without contradiction.

The question is then asked whether the method of division or dichotomy (used by Plato in the *Sophistes* in defining a Sophist as an orator or rhetorician), is useful or not. It is answered by Averroes in the affirmative, but only in those cases where the divisions of the *definiendum* are known, or else one would be involved in *petitio principii* or a vicious circle. That induction, which determines the universal by reference to its individual or particular instances, is useful in formulating definitions, is denied by Averroes. However, in defining an entity, we must first determine whether it exists or not by recourse to induction; otherwise we would have a purely nominal or verbal statement of what the entity in question is, as when we describe a goat-stag, as a fictitious animal made up of two parts, a goat and a stag.[8]

Averroes concludes by asserting that the first principles of demonstration or definition are known through a faculty or disposition in us which rises from the lowest level of sense-perception, through the imagination and memory to the highest level of *intellectual* apprehension of the first principles of demonstration. These principles are by definition more certainly known to us than demonstrations themselves. It is for this reason that the intellect, or the faculty of apprehending those first principles, may be regarded as the principle of principles.

Having defined scientific knowledge as knowledge that the thing exists, coupled with the knowledge of the cause or causes whereby it exists, and having asserted that this knowledge culminates in the apprehension of the first principles upon which this knowledge ultimately rests, in an intuitive manner, Averroes turns to the discussion of the four causes, without the knowledge of which scientific knowledge is impossible. He asserts that each of these causes can be taken as a middle term of a demonstration. The material cause may be taken as the middle term of a demonstration, in so far as the middle

8. *Ibid.*, p. 461.

term is analogous to the matter of a demonstration and is common to both the major and the minor terms. Thus, if it is asked, why does the animal perish, the answer would be that it is made up of contraries. The formal cause may be taken as a middle term too; so that if one were to ask: 'Why is the angle of a triangle, inscribed in a semi-circle and tangential to the circumference, a right angle?', the answer would be because it is equal to the other two angles of that triangle. An example of the efficient cause used as a middle term is: 'Why did the People of the Camel (that is, 'Ai'ishah, al-Zubayr and the other partisans) fight 'Ali Ibn Abī Ṭālib in the so-called Battle of the Camel (in 656)?' the answer would be because of the murder of 'Uthmān, the third caliph. The final cause is used as middle term, also; so that if we ask: 'Why do physicians recommend walking before lunch and after dinner?' – the answer is for the sake of health. Here, Averroes observes, the difference between the efficient and the final causes is that the former precedes the effect in point of time, whereas the latter succeeds it in time.

Critique of al-Fārābī

It is well-known that al-Fārābī was the first Muslim logician, who wrote extensive paraphrases of or commentaries on all Aristotle's logical treatises. As the heir of the Greek–Arab philosophical tradition, Averroes is often concerned to comment on or criticize al-Fārābī for departing from the Aristotelian path in logic. Thus, speaking of Aristotle's *Analytica Posteriora* (*Kitāb al-Burhān*), Averroes is critical of al-Fārābī (Abu Nasr) for "rearranging the words of that book and the rules of demonstrative definitions."[9] This is confirmed by the modern edition of al-Fārābī's *Kitāb al-Burhān*, when compared with Aristotle's *Analytica Posteriora*.

Other instances of Averroes' criticisms of al-Fārābī may be mentioned. Thus, he criticizes al-Fārābī's distinction in the *Categories* between the universal aspect of the accident, such as whiteness, which is knowable, and the particular aspect, such as white, which is unknowable, in so far as this distinction is part of the definition of the subject. For Averroes, Aristotle

9. Ibn Abi Usaybi'ah, '*Uyūn al-Anbā*', p. 533.

states explicitly that the definition of the accident is not equivalent to the definition of the subject.[10]

With respect to 'mixed deductions,' Averroes criticizes al-Fārābī for 'imagining' that the major possible premise contains the condition which, according to al-Fārābī, is predicable of the whole in all the categories. For Averroes, both al-Fārābī and Alexander (of Aphrodisias) are in error in their interpretation of Aristotle on this point.[11]

As regards the possible in general, Averroes agrees with al-Fārābī's concept of definition in the first figure, but disagrees with him regarding the composition of existential and possible premises, in which the conclusion is universal. Aristotle held, according to Averroes, that if the major premise is necessary and the minor possible, the conclusion will not be universal, contrary to the syllogism in which the major premise is possible. He believes that this conclusion is obvious by induction. Thus, if we say that it is possible for every human to walk, that would be true of every human both in potentiality and in actuality; but if we say 'every human must walk,' that statement would only be true of every human who actually exists.

Similarly, Averroes was critical of al-Fārābī's argument that conditional syllogisms are sound or necessary on the ground that their necessity is part of the second or minor premise. Averroes objects that necessity is not part of the syllogism, but a subsidiary property thereof. Were the conditional syllogism sound on that ground, as al-Fārābī claims, we could have a sound syllogism which is made up of a single premise. Thus from the statement, for instance: 'If the sun is up, it is day,' we could infer inductively that it is day, or alternatively: 'It is not day, then the sun is not up.' Similarly, we could infer from the statement 'it is not night' that it is day; or from the statement 'it is day' that it is not night.[12] Here Averroes appears to be critical of the 'propositional constructions', which Aristotle overlooked in his logic and which were introduced subsequently by Zeno of Citium and the Stoics, as part of their propositional logic.

It is noteworthy that in all those cases in which al-Fārābī diverges from Aristotle, Averroes invariably takes the side of Aristotle, to whom

10. *Talkhīs Mantiq Aristu* I, p. 18.
11. *Ibid.*, p. 182.
12. *Ibid.*, p. 235.

he refers in his paraphrase of *Analytica Priora* (*Kitāb al-Qiyās*) in these hyperbolic terms of praise: "How wonderful is this man and how different is his nature from human natures generally. It is as though divine art (*sinā'ah*) brought him forth so as to inform us, humans, that ultimate perfection is possible in the human species perceptibly and demonstrably. Such [a person] is not human, that is why the ancients used to call him divine."[13]

Rhetoric and Poetics

In addition to the six traditional parts of the *Organon*, Averroes has commented on or paraphrased the *Rhetorica* and the *Poetica*, which were regarded as part of the *Organon* in the Arabic and Syriac traditions, as already mentioned. The reason, he gives, is that, like dialectic (*jadal*), the aim of rhetoric is persuasion, which Aristotle had acknowledged in *Rhetoric* I, 1355a14. Here he states that persuasion, which is the business of both dialectic and rhetoric "is clearly a sort of demonstration." Al-Fārābī fully concurred with this sentiment of Aristotle in his rhetorical works.[14] To illustrate his point, Averroes refers to al-Fārābī's classification of the four forms of government given in Aristotle's *Rhetorica* I, 8, i.e. democracy, oligarchy, aristocracy and monarchy, and tends to agree with his views regarding the relation of rhetoric to politics in which persuasion is used effectively. This view was probably given in al-Fārābī's lost work, the *Large Commentary on Rhetorica*. In his extant *Book of Letters* (*Kitāb al-Hurūf*), al-Fārābī even gives a historical account of the development of the 'persuasive arts,' starting with rhetoric, followed by dialectic and culminating in demonstration, which is the 'subtlest' of these arts.[15]

With respect to poetry, Averroes and al-Fārābī are in agreement that poetical discourse is a form of logical discourse, since it is concerned with imitation (*muhākāt, mimesis*), which is analogous to science in demonstration, opinion in dialectic and persuasion in rhetoric. It follows that poetics

13. *Ibid.*, p. 213.
14. Cf. al-Fārābī, *Deux ouvrages inédits sur la rhétorique*, p. 31.
15. *Kitāb al-Hurūf*, p. 132.

is a branch of logic, in so far as it is concerned with 'imaginative' and 'imitative' discourse which is liable to truth or falsity.[16]

Despite the concurrence of these two brilliant logicians, to whom the name of Avicenna should be added, it is significant that they all tended to follow in the footsteps of earlier, probably Syriac logicians. For although rhetoric, which is concerned with persuasion, may be affiliated to logic, the case of poetics, we believe, is different. For Aristotle is categorical that the function of the poet differs from that of the logician, whose discourse is susceptible of truth and falsity, affirmation and negation. The function of the poet, he writes: "is to describe, not the thing that happened, but a kind of thing that might happen; i.e. what is possible as being probable or necessary."[17] Thus, the difference between the poet and the historian, he adds, is not that one writes in verse and the other in prose, but rather that one describes events as they *have* happened, and the other events as they *might* happen. For this reason, he regarded poetry as more philosophical than history and its aim, expressed in the form of imagination or imitation, is artistic pleasure or *catharsis*, i.e. the purgation of the soul from the emotions of pity or fear. This is particularly true of the highest forms of poetry, tragic and epic poetry, which consist of "being an imitation of serious subjects in a grand verse." Of the two, tragedy is the nobler, since it is "an imitation of an action that is serious and also as having magnitude, complete in itself; in language with pleasurable accessories, each kind brought in separately in the parts of the work; in a dramatic, not in a narrative form; with incidents arousing pity and fear, wherewith to accomplish its *catharsis* of such emotions."[18]

By asserting that the aim of tragedy, as well as other forms of poetry, is dramatic effect, or in a broader sense the purgation of emotions, rather than narrative report, as in the case of history, Aristotle clearly intended to assign poetry to a region higher than, or at least different from, logical discourse, whether demonstrative or persuasive.

---

16. *Talkhīs Kitab al-Shi'r,* p. 58.
17. *Poetics,* 1451a 37 f.
18. *Ibid.* 1449b 24 f.

5

The Physical Structure of the Universe

The Aristotelian Physical Corpus

Aristotle's philosophy of nature is embodied in a series of treatises, headed by the *Physics*. This treatise was known in the Arabic sources as the *Book of Physical Hearing (physike akroasis)*, in reference to Aristotle's acroamatic, or oral, instruction at the Lyceum. To the *Physics* should be added the *Generation and Corruption*, the *Meteorology, De Coelo* and the *Substantia Orbis*, on all of which Averroes has commented or paraphrased.

He opens the *Paraphrase of the Physics* by declaring his intention to discuss the 'scientific' statements found in that work, to the exclusion of the historical references of Aristotle to his predecessors, in so far as they do not bear directly on the substance of the physical enquiry, or are purely dialectical. Another reason why he was anxious to expound Aristotle's physical views accurately, we are told, is that some writers, of whom he mentions al-Ghazālī in his famous *Intentions of the Philosophers (Maqāsid al-Falāsifah)* had aimed at that goal but failed.

Apart from this polemical observation, Averroes argues next that whoever is interested in the study of physics must first acquaint himself with logic, as we have seen in the previous chapter. He then proceeds to assert, as he has done in logic, that scientific or certain knowledge of any entity consists in knowing its primary causes, followed by its proximate causes and the elements or components making it up.

The order of instruction to be followed in this science, he goes on to argue, consists in starting with matters which are better known to us, regardless of whether they are better known by nature or not. These matters include general principles, which are characteristic of particulars, rather than universals. For this reason, according to Averroes, Aristotle begins by defining nature, then proceeds to discuss the first principles of physical entities; namely, Prime Matter and the First Mover. As for the first forms and the ultimate purpose underlying natural processes, their discussion belongs, according to him, to a 'higher science,' which he identifies with the 'universal art' or first philosophy, i.e. metaphysics. The chief aim of physics is then given as the investigation of movable entities and the purposes they seek, in so far as they are movable. Notwithstanding, Aristotle begins by the discussion of Prime Matter, according to Averroes, because it is the most obvious primary cause of physical entities. The ancients, by whom he no doubt meant the Presocratic or Ionian philosophers, starting with Thales and ending with Empedocles, as Aristotle states in *Physics* I, 6 f., tended to begin likewise with matter.

If the subject-matter of physics is movable entities, as already mentioned, it behooves the physicist, then, to enquire into the varieties of motion to which such entities are liable. Thus, these entities are subject to change or alteration, which is a species of motion, and is of two types: 1) accidental, which inheres in a subject, and 2) substantial, which transforms the individual entity, as the bearer of change or generation, totally. The former requires a substratum or matter (*hayūlā*), the latter an analogous substance preceding it, since nothing comes to be out of nothing or out of any subject haphazardly. Were it possible for a thing to come out of nothing or haphazardly, it would have been possible for rust, for instance, to come from non-copper and a learned scholar from a non-learned scholar, which is absurd. In the processes of change or generation, he believes, nature follows a uniform pattern.

The part of the entity which changes, he goes on to explain, is the form; whereas the part which remains unchanged is matter. That part which does not change, i.e. matter, is obviously not subject to generation or corruption, but only alteration or transformation (*istihālah*). Hence, it is necessary to posit an ultimate subject of generation and corruption, which is potentially all things and which does not exist in actuality apart from form. This subject or substratum is Prime Matter, which is equivalent to pure potentiality, or the disposition for the endless reception of forms in succession. Nevertheless, it is different from privation (*'adam*), in so far as privation is purely accidental, unlike Prime Matter which is the essential pre-condition of generation and corruption.[1]

In the *Jawāmi' Kitāb al-Kawn wa'l-Fasād* (*Epitome of Generation and Corruption*), Averroes pursues the discussion of this double notion of form and matter, as well as in *Meteorologica*, Book IV. Here, we are told, Aristotle has given an account of the way in which all physical entities derive from the *homoemera*, or entities of similar parts, i.e. inorganic substances, from which entities of dissimilar parts or organic substances arise. In *De Coelo*, we are further told, Aristotle discusses the four elements and the processes of their transformation into each other, on which he has dwelt in the *Epitome of Generation and Corruption*. This transformation is said to be motion in the category of substance, or transition from not-being to being. It differs from other forms of motion, such as growth or alteration, in that its subject is changed substantially and totally. Here he criticizes the ancient philosophers, by whom he meant the Presocratic naturalists, for not distinguishing between generation, as substantial change, and other forms of quantitative or qualitative change. Some of them posited one element, such as air, from which, through rarefaction and condensation, as Anaximenes actually held, generation and corruption take place in succession; others, such as Democritus and the atomists, reduced generation and corruption to the endless process of aggregation and segregation of the atoms from which physical components arise.[2]

A general maxim of Aristotelian physical theory is then discussed. Simple bodies, by which he means the four elements, of air, water, fire and earth, are said not to be susceptible of all the forms of change to which physical compounds are subject. For they are not susceptible of growth, but are susceptible of the remaining three, i.e. locomotion, alteration, and generation or corruption. The heavenly bodies, by contrast, are not subject to any form of motion or change, except locomotion. It follows,

1. *Jawāmi' al-Samā' al-Tabī'i*, in *Rasā'il Ibn Rushd*, p. 16.
2. *Jawāmi 'al-Kawn wa'l Fasad*, p. 114. Cf. Aristotle, *De Gen. et Corrup.* I, 314b.

according to Averroes, that the heavenly bodies are incorruptible and everlasting, simple and fully actual. Unlike physical bodies, they are also animate or moved by a soul, as Avicenna had also taught in his attempt to explain their particular motions. The reason Averroes gives is that the circular motions of the heavenly bodies are only possible through the soul, which is the principle of desire. The four elements, by contrast, are subject to the upward and downward motions proper to each, fire and air moving upwards, water and earth moving downwards.

Moreover, unlike physical objects, the heavenly bodies are not made up of form and matter, and therefore are not located in a particular place (*topos*), which is a characteristic of physical objects only. Their motion is eternal or unceasing, since they are ungenerable and incorruptible, by reason of the fact that they are not made up of form and matter, as already mentioned, but are entirely simple. Their eternal and circular motion is caused by an intellect or intelligence (*'aql*), which is analogous to man's intellect. In fact, to each heavenly body corresponds a separate or immaterial intellect, which moves by the force of desire emanating from its soul. The object of this desire is the noblest and the best, which, in the last analysis, is the ultimate mover of the universe, called by Aristotle the Unmoved Mover. Like the Unmoved Mover, it is characteristic of the heavenly bodies to know themselves, as well as everything beneath them.[3] However, the Unmoved Mover (or God) is pre-eminent in that its knowledge embraces the knowledge of all things, including Itself as the final cause of the universe, which the heavenly bodies cannot apprehend. It is in this ingenious way that Averroes solves the problem of the Unmoved Mover's knowledge of inferior entities, of which He is the cause.

In the *Meteorology*, known in Arabic as *Talkhīs al-Āthār al-'Ulawiyah*, Averroes discusses that region which is intermediate between the terrestrial and the celestial regions. After reviewing the views of the various Peripatetics, including Alexander of Aphrodisias, he concludes that this region, which lies above the sublunary world of generation and corruption, is fiery in essence. By contrast, the celestial world, as the

---

3. *De Subs Orbis* III and V; *De Coelo et Mundo*, fo. 115. Cf. Rénan, *Averroès*, pp. 120 f.

Peripatetics generally taught, was made up of a fifth element, called ether (*athīr*).[4] In the sequel, he discusses the various meteorological phenomena, such as rain, wind, lightning, thunder, comets, earthquakes, etc., and concludes, in Book IV, with the discussion of the four elements, and the four primary qualities corresponding to them, i.e. hot and cold, moist and dry.

In the *Paraphrase of the Physics*, Averroes discusses natural entities or occurrences, as distinct from artificial entities or occurrences, on the one hand, and those which are the product of spontaneity or chance, on the other. What distinguishes natural entities from the artificial is that they have in themselves the principle of motion or rest. Some, such as animals, have in themselves the four forms of motion or change, locomotion, growth, alteration, and generation or its opposite, i.e. corruption. Nature is then defined along Aristotelian lines, as "a principle or cause of motion and rest inhering in the thing primarily and essentially." What distinguishes physical entities from artifacts and products of chance or spontaneity is then stated to be the fact that, unlike physical entities, the principles of their motions are accidental and extrinsic, rather than essential or intrinsic.

Here Averroes criticizes Avicenna for holding that the above Peripatetic definition of nature is inadequate, contending in addition that it belongs to the adept of metaphysics, rather than physics, to define it adequately. Now, Averroes comments, if Avicenna means by this remark that it is the business of the metaphysician to rebut the arguments purporting to prove that the existence of nature is not self-evident, then he is right. However, if he means that the existence of nature is not known in physics, but is demonstrated in metaphysics (as Avicenna actually claimed), then he is wrong. The existence of nature, as manifested in natural entities, is self-evident and does not require any demonstration, according to Averroes.[5]

What determines the nature of physical entities, he then explains, is their form rather than their matter. For, it is by virtue of their form that such entities are what they are and acquire the specific actions proper to

4. *Talkhīs al-Āthār al-'Ulawiyah*, pp. 25 f.
5. *Jawāmi' al-Samā' al-Tabī'i*, in *Rasā'il Ibn Rushd*, p. 22.

them, matter being simply the common or universal substratum of all physical entities.

The difference between the physicist and the mathematician, as far as the material cause is concerned, is next discussed. The physicist, he explains, investigates natural entities, in so far as they are made up of matter and form, as well as their agent and the purpose pertaining to them. The mathematician, on the other hand, investigates physical bodies or solids, planes, figures and points, in so far as they are separate from matter. He does not concern himself with questions of agency or purposiveness, in so far as these entities are independent of motion or change.

As for the purpose or final cause, it is clear, argues Averroes, that all existing entities, whether artificial or natural, tend towards the form as their proximate purpose and beyond it towards the "ultimate purpose of the universe as a whole." Like Aristotle, by this ultimate purpose he certainly meant the Unmoved Mover, or God, who is the actuality of thought and perfection, as Aristotle states in *Metaphysics* XII, 7.

To natural and artificial entities should be added, according to both Aristotle and Averroes, entities which arise by spontaneity or chance. Those entities tend to occur rarely, rather than for the most part, as natural entities tend to do. They are, therefore, fortuitous, as happens, for instance, when a person on digging a well chances to find a treasure, or when a rock happens to fall on someone's head and causes it to crack. None of those occurrences is the natural consequence of the action leading to it, except accidentally. Thus chance is a cause in an accidental, not an essential, sense and spontaneity is a cause in an undetermined or unpredictable sense.

Motion, the Infinite and Time

A large part of the *Paraphrase of the Physics* deals with motion, which together with matter is the chief distinguishing characteristic of natural entities, as we have seen. Having defined nature as a principle of motion or rest, it is necessary, Averroes argues, to define motion; but in so far as motion is continuous and infinite, it is the business of the physicist to define those two concepts also. To these concepts should be added space and time which the motion of natural entities presupposes necessarily.

The method adopted by Averroes in defining motion is that of division or dichotomy, rather than composition, because motion does not fall under any single one of the ten categories, but is found to exist in a number of ways. 1) In the category of position, it exists as locomotion; 2) in that of quality, as alteration; 3) in that of quantity, as increase or decrease; and 4) in that of substance, as generation or corruption. Its highest genus is the existent, which is divisible into that which exists in potentiality or possibility on the one hand, and in actuality or perfection on the other. For this reason, Averroes states, Aristotle has defined motion as "the perfection (or actuality) of that which is in potentiality, in so far as it is in potentiality."[6] For him, potentiality is "the specific differentia of motion, which ensures the continuity of its existence, in the same way that the differentia of existing entities ensure the continuity of their existence."[7] By this Averroes obviously means that potentiality is the distinctive characteristic of motion, as it is predicated of a movable entity and without which that entity would cease to exist qua movable.

In the discussion of the infinite, Averroes distinguishes, like Aristotle, between what may be increased *ad infinitum* and what may be divided *ad infinitum*. The former may be predicated of motion, time and generation or corruption; since they can be imagined to increase *ad infinitum*. In the latter sense, infinity may be predicated of time, in so far as it can be imagined to extend *ad infinitum*. A third meaning of the infinite is the metaphorical or figurative, according to which voice, for instance, may be said to be invisible and the sea infinite, in the sense that they cannot be circumscribed.

In general, what exists in actuality, such as place or space, which are by definition finite, cannot be infinite according to Aristotle, so that the outermost limits of the universe, however vast, must be regarded as finite. It was a fundamental postulate of Aristotelianism that the actual is always finite.

In the discussion of time, Averroes recognizes its close association with motion, so much so that where we are unable to conceive of motion we

6. Aristotle, *Physics* III, 201a 10.
7. *Jawāmi al-Samā'*, in *Rasā'il Ibn Rushd*, p. 31.

are unable to conceive of time. More specifically, when we do not perceive motion, we do not perceive time, as is related about the Sleepers of Ephesus, or the Sleepers of Sardinia referred to by Aristotle, or the People of the Cave, mentioned in the Qur'an. Averroes simply refers in this connection to "some ascetics" (*muta' allihūn*). That time is not identical with motion is declared by him to be self-evident; it is simply an accident of motion which is given in its definition as a part thereof. For we cannot imagine time apart from motion, although we can imagine motion apart from time. It is particularly apprehended in relation to locomotion, whose parts are conceived as prior and posterior. Prior and posterior are, in fact, aspects of past and future, which are separated by a boundary or limit, identified by Aristotle as the 'now.' That is why when we are not conscious of the 'now,' we are not conscious of time, in so far as we are not conscious of prior and posterior, before and after. It follows that our apprehension of time is bound up with our apprehension of the divisions of motion, by means of prior and posterior. That is why Aristotle has defined time as the number of motion, with respect to prior and posterior.[8]

In the shorter *Epitome of the Physics*, Averroes reiterates the Aristotelian maxim that all natural entities are made up of matter and form, then proceeds to define matter (*hāyūla*), by which he obviously meant Prime Matter, as "the ultimate substratum of all generable and corruptible entities, which is entirely free of actuality or specific form."[9] In that sense, matter is equivalent to that potentiality which lies at the basis of all natural entities, without being any one of them. Matter is, therefore, the first physical principle of all existing entities, although in itself it does not exist except in conjunction with form, which is the principle of 'the substantiation' of matter and, contrary to Plato's view, does not exist separately from matter, except in thought.

Prime Matter and Material Compounds

Prime Matter is neither generable nor corruptible. For, it is impossible to suppose that it was generated from another matter into which it is

---

8. *Ibid.*, p. 61. Cf. Aristotle, *Physics* IV, 219b 2.
9. Al-Samā' al-Tabī'i, in *Rasā'il Ibn Rushd*, p. 10.

corrupted, or else that matter would have come from another matter and so on *ad infinitum*. This would render generation and corruption impossible, due to the impossibility of the infinite regress.

The first physical entities to arise from Prime Matter are the four elements of water, fire, air and earth and the four primary qualities of hot and cold, moist and dry corresponding to them. Compound bodies arise from the four elements, by virtue of the action of those primary qualities. Two of these qualities, i.e. hot and cold, are active, since they can cause bodies to coalesce, and two, i.e. moist and dry, are passive, since they can cause bodies to dissolve. All contrary qualities or properties are reducible to those four.

In more specific terms, the process whereby compounds arise from the simple elements is designated as combination or coalescence, whereby bodies differ according to the measure of the elements entering into their composition and giving rise, in the first instance, to bodies of similar parts, or inorganic compounds, and in the second instance, to bodies of dissimilar parts, or organic compounds.[10]

The Heavenly Bodies and the Separate Intelligences

Organic compounds constitute the parts of animals and plants, or living organisms in general, and mark the highest stage of perfection in the world of generation and corruption, beyond which lie the heavenly bodies, which are made up, as we have already mentioned, of the fifth element, ether. They differ from generable and corruptible entities in their simplicity, the perdurability of their circular motions and their indestructibility. In that respect, they may be regarded as the first causes or first principles of the lower generable and corruptible entities. The reason given by Averroes is that physical causes are not sufficient by themselves for the generation of physical entities. They require in addition the action of the heavenly bodies, according to Aristotle, or the Active Intellect, according to Avicenna, described for that reason as 'the giver of forms,' since all 'substantial forms' emanate from it, as already mentioned.

10. *Talkhīs Kitāb al-Kawn wa'l-Fasād*, pp. 4–5.

Of those heavenly bodies, the sun plays, according to Averroes, a primary role. Thus its motion in the ecliptic, in accordance with the succession of the four seasons, is the ultimate cause of the generation of most terrestrial entities, as well as the motions of the moon and the other planets of Ptolemaic cosmology. Its action on the terrestrial entities, however, is more patent and thus it is not excluded that the duration of those entities may be influenced by the rotations of the planets, as the astrologers assert.[11] It is noteworthy that al-Kindī was the first Muslim philosopher to accord a decisive role, in the generation of terrestrial entities, to the heavenly bodies. Al-Fārābī, who wrote a famous treatise on the subject of astrology, was rather critical of the extravagant claims of professional astrologers. Averroes is content, in this context, to note the claims of astrologers without dwelling on the subject.

The motions of the heavenly bodies depend ultimately, as Aristotle explains in *Physics* VIII, 10, on the first moved mover or the first heaven, which is located at the outermost limit or circumference of the universe. However, this first moved mover, or *primum mobile*, depends on a higher principle of motion who is unmoved, is entirely immaterial, has no magnitude or body, is indivisible and is always in actuality.

The manner in which the Unmoved Mover moves the first moved mover is by way of desire. It follows, as we have already mentioned, that it must have a soul or be animate (*mutanaffis*), because it is impossible that, although higher than animate entities in the lower world, it should be inanimate, as Alexander of Aphrodisias has argued. However, such a mover, although animate, does not possess the two faculties of sensation or imagination, but only the higher faculty of thought. For the first two faculties exist in the animate entities for the sake of survival, whereas the third exists for the sake of well-being or perfection. It follows that the motion of the first moved mover arises by virtue of "that desire which is caused by rational thought," whose object is the supreme good, identified by Aristotle with the Unmoved Mover or God.

The number of the subordinate movers corresponds, according to Averroes, to the number of the heavenly bodies which derive their

---

11. Cf. al-Kawn wa' l-Fasād, in *Rasā'il Ibn Rushd*, p. 29; *Tahāfut al-Tahāfut*, p. 492.

motions from those higher principles which Aristotle calls the separate intelligences. Their number is given by Averroes as 38 to correspond to the Ptolemaic cosmological scheme, whereas Aristotle, basing himself on the astronomy of Eudoxus and Callipus, has given their number as 55, to correspond to the diurnal motions and counter-motions of the spheres.[12]

Averroes concludes this part of the discussion by observing that, since the motion of all the heavenly bodies is the same and is caused by a single mover, it follows that we can imagine the whole heavenly order "to constitute a single animal (*ḥayawān*) who is spherical in shape and whose outermost circumference is that of the sphere of fixed stars, and its core is in contact with the fiery orbit."[13] This orbit constitutes the highest orbit of the elements surrounding the earth, which is the center of the universe around which all the planets, including the sun and moon, rotate. Below the sphere of the moon, the orbits of the four elements surround the earth in a series of concentric circles, as the diagram below shows.

Having concluded the discussion of natural motions and the way in which, together with heavenly motions, they depend on the primary immaterial movers or 'separate intelligences,' Averroes proceeds to discuss the nature of these intelligences, about which Aristotle had spoken with the

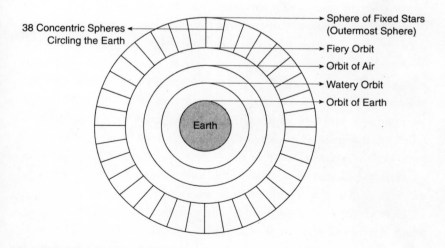

38 Concentric Spheres Circling the Earth

Sphere of Fixed Stars (Outermost Sphere)
Fiery Orbit
Orbit of Air
Watery Orbit
Orbit of Earth

Earth

12. *Metaphysics* XII, 1074a 10.
13. Mā Baʿd al-Tabīʿah, in *Rasāʾil Ibn Rushd*, p. 137.

greatest economy of words. To determine this nature, he explains, we should consider the nature of the intellect and its objects; namely, intelligible forms or universals discussed in psychology. This consideration reveals that the forms of natural entities are either sensible or intelligible. They are intelligible in so far as they are abstracted from matter and in the process are identified with the intellect; since, in the act of apprehending the universal, as Aristotle has taught, the object and the subject become one and the same. Being immaterial, the primary movers must be regarded as pure intellects or intelligences (*'aql*, *'uqūl*), too. As already mentioned, they move the heavenly bodies which are animate, as the object of desire moves the desirer or the beloved moves the lover, i.e. finalistically. This mode of motion, he then explains, is a form of intellectual conception or apprehension, which is entirely independent of the inferior faculties of sensation or imagination, which, as already mentioned, exist for the sake of mere survival. Being eternal and indestructible, the separate intelligences are not in need of that which contributes to their survival, but only their well-being or perfection, which is the function of intellectual faculties when fully actualized.

The relation of the separate intelligences to the heavenly bodies, Averroes further explains, is not confined to imparting the eternal, circular motions which belong to them in a finalistic manner, but the very forms whereby they are constituted. In that respect, they could be described as their agents, since agency is precisely the manner in which the form that constitutes the essence of the entity is imparted.

Next, he observes that those intelligible principles or substances, which move the heavens, although of one genus, differ in rank or pre-eminence. Thus some of them are prior in point of existence or immateriality, and as such are the causes of their lower counterparts. It follows that whichever of these intelligences is prior in the absolute sense must be "the ultimate cause of the existence of the rest." This ultimate cause is the Unmoved Mover or the First Principle of motion in the universe, as Aristotle has also concluded in the *Metaphysics*.

Here Averroes gives a proof of the existence of the First Principle, which may be called the argument from the hierarchy of being. The gist of this proof is that there is a necessary relation between immaterial principles or agents, by reason of the fact that the term 'principle' is applied to them all "by priority and posteriority," so that whatever principles are of this kind "must be referred necessarily to a single being, who is the cause of the existence of that property in them all."[14] Thus the term 'heat' is applied to fire and to hot things, not equivocally, but by priority and posteriority; so that fire is said to be hot by virtue of being the principle or cause of heat, whereas hot objects are said to be hot by virtue of receiving heat from fire.

Another chief characteristic of those immaterial intelligences is that they are able to apprehend themselves, just as our own intellects do, not directly, but rather indirectly through the apprehension of other intelligences. However, they do not apprehend their effects; because were they to apprehend what is beneath them, "the superior would depend for its perfection on the inferior" and then the apprehensions of the higher intelligences would be subject to generation and corruption, like their inferior objects, which is absurd.

This last statement appears to be contradicted by what Averroes asserts in the *Substantia Orbis*, *De Coelo* and the *Tahāfut*.[15] For here he asserts that the heavenly bodies, as well as the intelligences which move them, apprehend themselves, "as well as what is beneath them," or the whole order of generable and corruptible entities, who, as we have seen, derive their motion from them. Only the Unmoved Mover is spared by Aristotle the indignity of apprehending what is inferior to it. For Averroes, however, the First Principle cannot, in the light of the overwhelming Qur'anic conception of God as the All-knowing, All-powerful Creator of the world, be regarded as ignorant of or indifferent to the fate of His creation. In the very act of knowing Himself, as we will see in a forthcoming chapter, God knows the totality of inferior and superior entities of which He is the cause, by dint of the same act of knowing Himself as their cause.

14. *Ibid.*, p. 146.
15. *Tahāfut al-Tahāfut*, p. 500. Cf. Rénan, *Averroès*, p. 122.

6

The Soul and its Faculties

Generation of Organic Compounds

For Aristotle, psychology formed part of the physical sciences, whereas his master Plato regarded the soul as a denizen of the Intelligible World which was fated by reason of some inexplicable fault to descend into the body of animals and plants, but only for a while. Aristotle, essentially a realist, regarded the soul, as he has put it in *De Anima* II, as the "first perfection (*entelecheia*) of an organic body capable of life;" in other words, the culmination of the biological process, which is essentially grounded in the body.

Averroes begins his discussion of the soul by recalling the main conclusions reached in the science of physics, of which, as already mentioned, the study of the soul is a part. Thus he recalls Aristotle's thesis that all generable and corruptible entities are made up of matter and form. Prime Matter, itself the ultimate substratum of becoming, does not exist unless it is 'informed' and, as such, is actually synonymous with pure potentiality.

From bodies made up of similar parts, as a result of the combination of the four elements, as we have seen in a previous chapter, arise bodies of dissimilar parts, or animal organs, by way of 'concoction' caused by 'natural heat,' which is the principle of life in all living organisms. The reader is referred in this context to the *Meteorology*, and the *Book of Animals*, as the zoological corpus in nineteen books, known to the Arabs, was called.

Both animals and plants, he then explains, receive their shapes and 'humorous' forms from this natural heat, or principle of life, subsisting in the seed or the semen, where species capable of procreation are conceived. Species not capable of procreation receive their forms from the heavenly bodies. However, in both animals and plants the nutritive faculty which is the primary faculty, common to all living organisms, is the direct cause of their natural shapes and forms. More specifically, it is derived from its like in another animal or plant. However, its ultimate cause is the separate intelligence, which Averroes does not name, but which the Muslim Neoplatonists, with Avicenna at their head, had identified with the Active Intellect, called for that reason the Giver of Forms (*Wāhib al-Ṣuwar*), as we have mentioned in a previous chapter.

As the primary faculty of the soul, the nutritive faculty may be regarded as the substratum of the higher faculties in the animal, starting with sensation and culminating in reason as far as man is concerned. However, the relation of these higher faculties to the nutritive may be described as one of fulfilment or perfection, in so far as they fulfill nature's urge to rise higher and higher, from the lowest to the highest faculties of the soul in a hierarchical manner.

Compared to material forms, the soul is clearly different from any of them, in so far as it does not possess any of their specific attributes. It is therefore a form of a specific kind, which Averroes describes as the form or first perfection of a natural body. Such a perfection differs from secondary perfection, as possession differs from exercise. Thus, when the animal is asleep and not actively exercising its powers, it still possesses soul as a disposition, which can be fully actualized when it is awake.[1]

The Five Faculties of the Soul

The perfections of the soul correspond to the five powers or faculties of the soul, the vegetative or nutritive, the sensitive, the imaginative, the rational and the appetitive. The higher faculty always presupposes the lower in such a way that they all depend on the nutritive, which is the

1. *Talkhīs Kitāb al-Nafs*, Nogales, p. 18.

precondition of life and growth. The function of that faculty is to turn nutrients from a state of potentiality to a state of actuality, and may be regarded for that reason as an active power. Its tool or instrument is the natural heat, which acts by way of mixture or combination, ensuring thereby the survival of the plant or animal. For, the bodies of animate entities are subtle or rarefied, and accordingly easily dissolved. If the animal or plant did not have a faculty capable of replacing what is dissolved, it would not be able to survive for long.[2]

Closely related to the nutritive faculty is the faculty of growth, to which the reproductive faculty is related. This faculty differs from the nutritive in that it produces out of what is an individual potentially an individual actually; whereas the nutritive produces part of an individual only. Similarly, its function, which is reproduction, is not fulfilled without the assistance of a mover from outside, which is the heavenly body, according to Aristotle, and the Active Intellect, according to Avicenna. However, this faculty is not essential or necessary for the survival of animate entities, like the nutritive faculty and the faculty of growth. It exists rather by way of supererogation, "so that those (animate) entities may have a share in eternal perdurance, to the extent their natures allow."[3] That is why it is possible for the former two faculties to exist in animals and plants without the reproductive, and for the nutritive to exist without the faculty of growth. However, none of these faculties can exist without the nutritive, which is the essential pre-condition of life and whose absence spells out the death of the animate entity.

External Senses

Next in the order of progression comes the sensitive faculty, which Averroes describes as a passive power, contrary to the nutritive which is active. Its two divisions are the proximate and the ultimate. The mover of the ultimate part of this faculty, which resides in the embryo and brings it into actuality, is the heavenly body; whereas its proximate mover is the actually sensible object.

2. *Ibid.*, p. 26.
3. *Ibid.*, p. 29.

The sensitive faculty exists in animals in which the nutritive faculty has reached the highest degree of perfection, but not in plants. Its action consists in abstracting the particular forms, such as colors and sounds, from their material substrata and raising them to a higher level of immateriality.

It is characteristic of the sensitive faculty that it is sometimes in potentiality, sometimes in actuality, and is therefore generable and corruptible. Were it everlasting, like the rational faculty, as we will see shortly, the sensible forms would exist in it prior to their actual existence upon being abstracted from their material substrata; and then sensible forms or properties, which are mere accidents, would be everlasting, which is absurd. Moreover, this faculty cannot exist apart from matter and cannot dispense with bodily organs, as the rational faculty can.

The first of the sensible faculties and the most primary is the sense of touch, which Aristotle had described as the 'sense of food' and regarded as the precondition of the survival of the animal.[4] It is so general that it may exist apart from the other senses, as shown by marine sponges and those other organisms which are intermediate between animals and plants, and which Aristotle has called zoophytes, or plant–animals, adding to this category sea-coral in the *Generation of Animals*, Book II. By contrast, none of the other senses can exist apart from touch, which may be regarded for that reason as their essential precondition.

The faculty of touch is actualized by tangible objects, which are of two kinds: 1) primary tangibles, which correspond to the four primary qualities of hot and cold, moist and dry; and 2) secondary tangibles, which are generated by the former, such as hardness, softness and other contrary qualities.

The organ of this faculty, of which no animal is divested, is the flesh. For Averroes, this flesh is not the medium of touch, as Themistius held, nor the same as the nerves, as Galen held, since the latter are not simple and are distributed throughout the whole body. Instead, he holds that the substratum of the sense of touch is the natural heat, which subsists in the heart and the arteries. Its organ perceives excessive qualities by means of

---

4. *De Anima* II, 414b 5.

the brain, which moderates natural heat; but since the nerves emanate from the brain, they must have a share in this function of the sense of touch. In this connection, Averroes rejects Galen's view, which is much closer to modern physiological theory, that the brain is the center of this sense or its source, clinging to the rival view of Aristotle that the center of sensation is the heart, whereas the brain is the organ which moderates the natural heat, as already mentioned.

The second sense is smell whose object is odors and whose medium is air or water. It is characteristic of smell that it belongs to objects which are tasteful, and thus smell and taste are often contiguous so that, from smell, tastes could be inferred in many cases. For this reason, Averroes defines taste "as the intermixture of dry with moist substances, by a sort of ripening (*nudj*)"[5] Similarly, smell also belongs to bodies in so far as these are mixed, contrary to colors and sounds, and subsist in both the object and the medium, which simply serves as the purveyor of the object smelt, when it is dissolved. That is why heat contributes to the dissemination of smell.

A basic difference between smell and taste is that the latter requires immediate contact with its object, and may be described on that account as a kind of touch. For this reason, some philosophers, like Alexander of Aphrodisias, have argued that this faculty, like touch, does not require a medium. Others have held instead that, since the tongue perceives tastes by means of the moisture found in the mouth, this moisture may be regarded as its medium. When this moisture is lacking, taste becomes impossible or hard, as Ibn Bājjah and Themistius, we are told, believed. Averroes' own view is that moisture is one of the tools or means of taste, rather than its medium.[6]

Next, vision is defined by Averroes, as "the faculty which receives the notions of color, as divested from matter, in so far as they are particular notions." To the extent it is not in contact with its object, it requires a medium, as is the case with hearing and smell. That is why, contrary to Democritus' view, vision is not possible in the void, or upon the contact of the visible object with the organ of vision. Averroes then goes on to

---

5. *Talkhīs Kitāb al-Nafs*, Nogales, p. 65. Cf. Aristotle, *Parts of Animals* II, 665b.
6. *Talkhīs Kitāb al-Nafs*, Nogales, p. 57.

explain that the body which receives color, although itself colorless, is the diaphanous medium,[7] which serves as the medium in which the colors of things subsist. However, this subsistence, to be complete, requires another agent which is light, an essential property of the heavenly bodies, but an accidental property of fire. Its essence, according to Averroes, is the perfection of the diaphanous ether in so far as it is diaphanous. However, to become actualized, vision presupposes a series of additional factors, which include distance from the lighted object and a certain magnitude proper to it; so that if the object is too close to the eye or is too small, it will not be seen; and if the light is inadequate, it will only be dimly perceived. He then explains that the act of lighting is one of those indivisible perfections which do not take place in time, and thus it is not a material or bodily form. Once the actually diaphanous body, which is fire or ether, mixes with non-diaphanous or opaque objects, color is generated. Therefore, color, he explains, is a kind of innate light actualized by external light, i.e. the light of the sun. Thus, the view that light gives the medium the disposition to receive color or actual transparency falls to the ground, since it presupposes that it lights the color in so far as it is lit – which is absurd.

Hearing, which is discussed next, is described as the sense which apprehends sounds emanating from colliding, hard objects, provided the motion of the object it collides with is faster than the dispersion of the air, which serves as the medium of hearing. Like vision, hearing is one of the senses which do not require contact with the object from which the sound emanates.

The Internal Senses

At this point, Averroes proceeds to distinguish between special and common sensibles, as well as the faculty or faculties which apprehend them. The chief characteristic of the former is that they are the objects of one faculty of sense, such as colors or sounds; whereas the latter are objects of two or more senses, and they include motion, rest, number, shape and magnitude. It is necessary, therefore, that there exist, besides

7. *Al-mushiff* or the transparent medium, which Aristotle identifies with ether.

the five special senses already discussed, a common faculty of sense which: 1) perceives the latter common sensibles; 2) discriminates between one sensible quality and another; and 3) perceives that it perceives.

Such a faculty, traditionally referred to as the *sensus communis*, must be one in one sense, and many in another. It is many in so far as it apprehends different sensibles by means of different organs, but one in so far as it apprehends the distinction of one sensible from another. It is thus one in essence, but many in relation to the organs involved, and may be compared, as Aristotle says, to the lines which emanate from the center of the circle to the circumference. Such lines are many in so far as they touch the circumference and one in so far as they converge on the center of the circle. Moreover, the mode of this faculty's apprehension of common sensibles is not entirely different from that of the other, special faculties of sense; since it receives the forms of sensibles as divested from their matter. Similarly, it is capable of apprehending contrary qualities at once, like the special senses, and is indivisible like them, in so far as it is not material or corporeal.

The *sensus communis*, Averroes goes on to explain, is analogous in some respects to other internal senses, such as the imagination, which is next discussed. He observes that some people, like Democritus, have identified the imagination with external sensation, whereas others, like Empedocles, have identified it with opinion. Plato, on the other hand, has held that it is a compound of opinion and sensation.

For Averroes none of those views is tenable. For him, imagination differs from sensations: 1) in so far as it apprehends objects which are no longer present, unlike the special senses, which apprehend their object only so long as it is present; 2) its apprehensions are often false or fictitious; and 3) we can produce by its means certain compound images of objects which we have only perceived separately. The latter is obviously a function of the creative imagination.

Imagination differs from opinion, on the other hand, in so far as its objects are voluntary, unlike the objects of opinion which are not, and in so far as opinion is susceptible of truth or falsity, contrary to the imagination. For, we can imagine things whose truth or falsity has not been determined yet. If this is the case, the third view, which attempts to combine both sensation and opinion, as Plato has done, falls to the ground, too.[8]

Next, Averroes examines the view, whose exponents are not named, that the imagination is a form of reasoning, and rejects it on the ground that the objects of the imagination and those of reason are not the same. The objects of the imagination are particular and material, whereas the objects of reason are universal and immaterial. It is also characteristic of the imaginative faculty that its action is subject to time, unlike the reasoning faculty. By this, Averroes appears to mean that rational activity can be instantaneous, as happens in the intuitive act; whereas the act of the imagination is often long-drawn.

Another argument adduced by him is that the imagination has a close relation to the *sensus communis* in so far as imaginative forms are ultimately derived from the vestiges of sensible forms stored in the latter faculty and are conjured up by the imagination at will. This is shown by the fact that the imagination does not exist apart from sensation, to which the *sensus communis* is attributed; whereas sensation may exist apart from the imagination, as witnessed in the case of the lower animals, which are devoid of the faculty of imagination.

Averroes enquires, next, about the mover of this faculty or the object which actualizes it. Of the two alternatives, that it is the sensible forms or their vestiges stored in the *sensus communis*, he selects the latter view, adding that it belongs to the imaginative faculty to combine or separate those vestiges as it pleases. He does not deny that the imaginative faculty, like the faculty of sense, is subject to generation and corruption. For it is originally potential but is actualized, as we have seen, by the vestiges of the sensitive forms stored in the *sensus communis*. It exists in some animals as the faculty that stimulates desire or appetite, which is the cause of their motion.[9] Thus the appetitive faculty causes the animal to seek the useful and shun the harmful, to the extent it is moved by the imagination. If the object of desire or appetite is pleasure, it is called passion (*shawq*); if vengeance, it is called anger; and if deliberation or reflection, it is called choice or will.

8. *Talkhīs Kitāb al-Nafs*, Nogales, pp. 83 f. and Plato, *Timaeus*, 52A and *Sophistes*, 264B.
9. *Talkhīs Kitāb al-Nafs*, Nogales, p. 89.

The relation of the appetitive faculty to the imaginative is so essential, that unless the animal imagines that a certain notion or property, pertaining to the object, is pleasurable or repugnant, it will not move towards or away from it, regardless of whether that object is present or absent. It follows, according to Averroes, that it is impossible for an animal capable of local motion to be devoid of imagination.[10] Here he draws a parallel between reason and the imagination, which is the principle of motion in animals devoid of reason, as against reason, which is the principle of motion in rational beings, but not without the assistance of the imagination.

Before we turn to the rational faculty, it may be appropriate to expound briefly Averroes' account of the two internal senses of memory and recollection, as given in his paraphrase of Aristotle's *Parva Naturalia*, known in the Arabic sources as *On Sense and the Sensible (al-Ḥiss wa'l-Maḥsūs)*, as already mentioned. This treatise formed part of Aristotle's psychology and consisted of the following parts: *On Memory and Recollection, On Slep and Prophesying by Dreams, On Length and Brevity of Life, On Youth and Old Age, On Life and Death and On Respiration.*

Averroes states explicitly in his paraphrase that the only four parts of *Parva Naturalia* to "be found in our country [i.e. al-Andalus]" are *On Sense and the Sensible, On Memory and Recollection, On Sleep and Prophesying by Dreams* and *On Length and Brevity of Life*. The first part repeats essentially what was said in *De Anima*, whereas the second engages in a lengthy discussion of memory and recollection. Here Averroes begins by defining the object of memory as that which has already occurred in the past, unlike recollection which he defines as the act of recalling, or conjuring up by an act of will and reflection, occurrences or entities which have been forgotten. Thus recollection is confined to mankind, unlike memory which is common to all higher animals capable of imagining. To those two modes of remembering or recollecting past events, Averroes adds the power of retention (*ḥifẓ*), which he defines as "the act of the soul whereby it retains what has been apprehended in the past up to the present."[11] In this respect, it differs from memory, which may lack this character of

10. *Ibid.*, p. 134.
11. *Talkhīs Kitāb al-Ḥiss wa' l-Maḥūs*, p. 37.

continuity and may have been suggested by the classic practice of retention, as applied to the Qu'ran or Arabic poetry.

The faculty of memory has a certain relation to the imagination, which is the faculty of apprehending those forms or notions proper to it at once; whereas, memory and recollection conjure up or retain those images for an extended period of time. Averroes comments on this difference by observing that sometimes we apprehend an imagined object without its form or vice versa, but we cannot retain many things by rote, without being able to imagine them, either because they are too strange or too incomprehensible. Moreover, because recollection is a willful act of conjuring up certain past notions or incidents, it is possible for one who is trying to recollect a certain notion or incident to fail, due to some deficiency of his internal powers, although it is possible for some people to imagine something they have not seen. Thus people who live in isolation, having cut themselves off from the world of sense, by whom Averroes obviously means mystics or ascetics, may be able to partake of strange imaginative experiences.[12]

Sleep is then defined as the declining of the *sensus communis*, whose functions of distinguishing, comparing and correlating sensations are interrupted, whereupon it recedes into the interior of the body.[13] Thus, when the powers of sense weaken in sleep, the cogitative power is strengthened, so that one will be able to apprehend future occurrences which one does not perceive in waking. The forms of such extra-sensuous experiences are given by Averroes as three: 1) visionary experience (*ru'ya*) due to the angels; 2) prognostication (*kahānah*), due to the jinn; and 3) inspiration emanating from God. Prophethood, which is a form of visionary experience, is referred to God and the angels. When the separate intelligence, by which Averroes meant the Active Intellect, imparts to "the imaginative soul the universal form of the particular event; I mean its intelligible cause, the imaginative soul is made to receive it in so far as it is embedded in matter, or to receive its intelligible form in reality. It might also be disposed to receive its likeness."[14] That is why

12. *Ibid.*, p. 46.
13. *Ibid.*, p. 67.
14. *Ibid.*, p. 79.

prophecies bear on concrete objects or occurrences, or on their
representations which are more akin to the nature of the universal.
Averroes was obviously trying to justify a fundamental aspect of his theory
of sensuous representations, addressed in Scripture (or the Qu'ran) to the
masses at large. For, of the two forms of the object of prophecy as
embodied in revealed Scripture, the corporeal and the 'figurative,' the latter
is clearly higher because it is of the nature of the universal. Accordingly, the
figurative representations used in Scripture are perfectly veridical, in fact
they are superior to the purely sensuous or corporeal representations
intended to appeal to the limited intelligence of the masses.

The Rational Faculty

When we come to the rational faculty, which marked, for both Aristotle
and Averroes, the capstone of the science of psychology, we are faced with
a series of problems, expressed in these three questions which Averroes
asks at the outset: 1) does this faculty exist or not; 2) how does it differ
from the other faculties of the soul; and 3) in what sense does it exist
sometimes in potentiality, sometimes in actuality. Once those three
questions are answered, we are told, we would be able to answer the more
complicated questions: 1) is the soul eternal or temporal; 2) is it material
or immaterial; and 3) what is the mover or agent who causes it to move
from potentiality to actuality? Those questions, or rather his answers to
them actually constitute the substance of Averroes' theory of reason or the
intellect.

The first general observation he makes is that the rational faculty
apprehends general notions in a universal way, unlike sense and the
imagination which apprehend them in a particular way and in so far as
they are embedded in matter. The rational faculty, by contrast,
apprehends general notions, as divested from matter, either by bringing
them together, as in conception (*taṣawwur*), or judging one in relation to
the other, as in assent or judgment (*taṣdīq*). Those two activities, as we
have seen in the discussion of logic, were the two major divisions of that
science in the Arabic tradition, but were really prefatory to the higher or
syllogistic division, also known as the analytic.

Teleologically speaking, Averroes then observes that, contrary to the other faculties which exist in the animal for the sake of its survival, the rational faculty has been placed in mankind for the sake of their perfection. It is for this reason that it is the basis of both the theoretical sciences and the practical arts, accessible to mankind, but not the lower animals. Hence its two divisions are the practical and the theoretical. The former bears on certain notions apprehended through sense-experience and derived ultimately from the two faculties of sensation and imagination. Although, as we have seen earlier, these two faculties are interdependent, the imagination plays a more decisive part in endowing mankind with those skills which enable them to produce certain artifacts of which the lower animals are not capable. Certain animals, however, such as bees which build their beehives and spiders which build their cobwebs, do so without reflection or deliberation; their artistic skills are purely instinctive.

Moreover, mankind apprehends, through the practical faculty, certain particular imaginative forms or phantasms which give rise to voluntary actions associated with practical or moral virtues, such as courage, friendship and love. The existence of such virtues is bound up with the ability to imagine in a particular way what ought to be done and to what extent.[15] Although Averroes does not mention it in this context, the practical faculty is the one with which ethical and political deliberation and action are bound up.

By contrast, the theoretical faculty apprehends general notions or intelligibles, in so far as they are universal, without reference to art, practical action or advantage. That is why it is important to investigate the nature of intelligibles, if we are to grasp the nature of the theoretical part of the rational faculty.

The first question that arises in connection with these intelligibles is whether they exist first in potentiality and subsequently in actuality, or whether they exist in actuality always, as Plato held. To answer this question, argues Averroes, it is necessary to examine the mode of our human relation to them. If this relation is analogous to that of the separate

15. *Ibid.*, p. 71.

intelligibles to matter, from which they are essentially distinct, although they could inhere in it, our acquisition of intelligibles would be independent of the conditions of life, and we would be able to apprehend them, first in potentiality and then in actuality. Thus, when the material impediments are removed and the appropriate intellectual stage, called the habitual, is attained, they will be revealed to us at once. It follows that we do not need an outside agent to cause them to be known by us, except accidentally. Our case in that respect is similar to that of the mirror, of which it may be said that whatever removes the rust is the cause of images being reflected in it.[16]   Averroes was obviously concerned in this connection to vindicate the essential efficacy of the intellect, against the Neoplatonists and the mystics (Sufis), who tended to conceive of it as passive, and accordingly dependent on some external source of 'illumination' (*ishrāq*), such as the Active Intellect, or God.

The difference between the particular, intelligible objects of the intellectual faculty and particular, material or sensible forms, is that the latter subsist in material entities, are multiple, are liable to change or alteration and are known through abstraction, which separates their forms from their matters. This is achieved progressively by means of sensation and the imagination. By contrast, universal intelligibles involve no plurality or composition and are independent of matter, so that the subject and object of thought in them is identical and thus they are known at once. In addition, the apprehension of particular forms is finite, whereas that of universal intelligibles is infinite.

Another characteristic of the intellectual faculty is that, unlike the sensitive, it is entirely free from passivity or liability to change and does not weaken, but rather increases with age.[17]   Despite those differences, Averroes recognizes the natural progression of the intellect from the lower to the higher stages of abstraction, due to its dependence on the two preliminary stages of sensation and imagination. "For we are compelled," he writes, "in acquiring [the intelligibles] to perceive at first, then imagine; whereupon, we are able to grasp the universal."[18]   The proof of

16. *Talkhīs Kitāb al-Nafs*, Nogales, p. 107.
17. *Ibid.*, p. 114.
18. *Ibid.*, p. 115.

this, as Aristotle has also argued in *De Anima* III, 432a7, is that whoever has lost a certain organ of sense, such as sight, is unable to apprehend intelligibles associated with colour. Moreover, whoever has not perceived the individual will not be able to apprehend the species; and finally, the universal is not acquired except in the sequel of repeated acts of sensation and imagination. This will refute, he states, Plato's claim that learning is a matter of recollection, whereby the soul simply recalls its original knowledge of universals (Ideas), prior to its descent into the body. Were this the case, we would be able to apprehend certain things of which we had never perceived the particular or individual instances, or could apprehend everything intuitively and without instruction. Then there would be no point in learning whatsoever.[19]

Having answered the question of how particular and universal intelligibles or forms differ from each other, Averroes proceeds to enquire about their existence. Being compounds of form and matter, the existence of particular forms is inseparable from matter. The *existence* of universals, paradoxical as it may sound, is organically bound up with their association with matter. For, as he has put it, "the existence of the universal, qua universal, consists in its being particular."[20] For the universal exists only in so far as it inheres in a particular, as its actual substratum; otherwise universals would exist outside the soul or in a world of their own, as Plato held. The Platonic view, Averroes argues in the *Paraphrase of the Metaphysics*, is shot through with difficulties and is useless, at any rate, in our attempt to account for the knowledge of particulars or demonstrate their existence. In this respect, Averroes remains thoroughly a realist.

Moreover, the arguments the Platonists adduce in support of their view of universals consist entirely of "poetical and enigmatic statements used in teaching the masses at large,"[21] in other words, lacking any genuine demonstrative force.

From the statement that universal intelligibles can only exist in particulars, Averroes infers that our apprehension of those universals is

19. *Ibid.*, p. 116.
20. *Ibid.*, p. 117.
21. Jawāmiʿ māʿ Baʿd al-Tabīʿah, in *Rasāʾil Ibn Rushd*, p. 48.

possible only through the intermediary of the imaginative forms (phantasms), which stem from the sensible forms which we had previously perceived. Otherwise, he says, my apprehension of intelligibles would be identical with yours, since it has nothing to do with perceiving or imagining the forms abstracted from their substrata, and "all Aristotle's sciences could be actually acquired by one who has not read any of his books."[22] Clearly, sense-experience plays a decisive role in the process of learning, as Aristotle also held, and this process is ultimately grounded in the act of abstracting the universal forms from their matter

The Material and Active Intellects

Particulars which are made up of form and matter differ from universals in other respects. They are liable to constant change or generation and corruption, although their forms are not, since they are in essence intelligible or universal intelligibles. However, these forms which exist permanently in the Active Intellect and are in fact identical with it, are not liable to change. However, the disposition to apprehend universal intelligibles must subsist in a subject necessarily, which cannot be a body nor an intellect. Therefore, it must be a soul, or a power in the soul to apprehend universals. As such, it could be designated as the possible or material intellect, whose immediate substratum is the imaginative form. This power is described by Aristotle as "a substance which is potentially all intelligibles, although in itself it is nothing."[23]

In the *Large Commentary on De Anima*, Averroes is more specific. He interprets Aristotle to mean that the material intellect does not possess any corporeal or material form and accordingly must be numerically one for all human beings. Moreover, it must be ungenerated and incorruptible; what is generated or corrupted being simply the particular intelligibles apprehended by it in succession.[24]

To actualize the potentialities of this material intellect, a mover or agent is needed. This mover is the Active intellect, which is also

---

22. *Talkhīs Kitāb al-Nafs*, Nogales, p. 118.
23. *Ibid.*, p. 124. Cf. *De Anima* III, 429b 30.
24. Cf. *Averrois Cordubensis Commentarium Magnum*, 5, pp. 406 f.

common to all mankind. It actualizes the former intellect by raising the imaginative forms stored in it to the highest degree of abstraction and causes them to pass thereby from a state of potentiality to a state of actuality. Thus, the first stage of actualization, known as the habitual intellect, arises. This intellect represents an intermediate mode of cognition, lying between pure potentiality and pure actuality. When the human intellect reaches the highest stage of actuality, it will not, as actual intellect, called the speculative by Averroes, apprehend intelligibles only, but will apprehend itself as well and achieve thereby the condition of conjunction (*ittisāl*) with the Active Intellect. When this condition is reached, the highest stage of intellection at the human level, known as the acquired intellect, is attained. This is "the perfection, fullness and actuality, to which the material intellect was originally merely disposed." It represents for that reason a supernatural, or extra-natural perfection, "which is one of nature's wonders."[25] Notwithstanding, Averroes concludes the discussion in the paraphrase of *De Anima* by dissociating himself from this 'error' into which he was originally induced by Ibn Bājjah. His further reading of Aristotle convinced him, as he says, that "the material intellect cannot be that substance which possesses that potentiality which is equivalent to something in actuality; I mean, one of the forms. For were this the case, it would be able to receive all forms."[26]

If we turn now to the Active Intellect, we will find that it has for Averroes two functions; the first is to apprehend itself as one of the separate intelligences which move the heavenly bodies, the second is to cause the intelligibles stored in the material intellect to pass from potentiality to actuality. The first of these functions is higher, since it constitutes its ultimate goal or perfection. Nevertheless, the Active Intellect has to the material intellect an essential relation; for it is to it what form is to matter; that is why, Averroes writes, "man is able to use it whenever he pleases; I mean to think."[27]

---

25. As in al-Ahwāni's edition of *Talkhīs Kitāb al-Nafs*, p. 95.
26. *Talkhīs Kitāb al-Nafs*, Nogales, p. 128.
27. Hal Yattasil bi'l-'Aql al-Hayūlāni al-'Aql al-Fa'āl, Appendix of al-Ahwani's edition of *Talkhīs Kitāb al-Nafs*, p. 121.

Averroes develops further the notion of the relation of the Active Intellect to the material intellect in the *Large Commentary on De Anima*. To prove the existence of an active intellect, to begin with, he draws on Aristotle's argument in *De Anima* III, 430a10 that, "since in every class of things, as in nature as a whole, we find two factors involved: 1) a matter which is potentially all particulars included in the class; and 2) a cause which is productive in the sense that it makes them all." In addition, there should also exist in the soul "an active intellect which causes that intellect which is in potentiality [i.e. the material intellect] to become an intellect in actuality."[28] Not only in nature, but in the soul, too, Averroes argues, those two parts of the intellect, to which should be added intelligible forms, must be said to exist. The mode of operation of the Active Intellect is further described as bringing the intelligibles in the material intellect, by means of the imaginative forms (phantasms), as we have seen, to a state of actuality. The Active Intellect, like its material counterpart, is finally stated to be one for the whole of mankind, is ungenerated, incorruptible and eternal.[29] However, as he repeatedly mentions, this Active Intellect is a 'power in the soul,' as Aristotle had also stated, not a supermundane agency of the type proposed by al-Fārābī and Avicenna, responsible for moving the sublunary world and serving as the 'storehouse' of intelligibles, as well as substantial forms. It has to the soul an essential relation, being to the material intellect, which is also a part of the soul, what form is to matter, as already mentioned. Otherwise, intellectual activity or thought would not be one of the essential perfections of the soul, but something purely accidental to it.

Thus the medieval controversy which pitted the Latin Averroists against their rivals in the thirteenth century rested to some extent on a misunderstanding of Averroes' intent. Thomas Aquinas, in his *De Unitate Intellectus, Contra Averroistas*, actually accuses Averroes' Latin followers (i.e. Averroistas), such as Siger of Brabant and Boethius of Dacia, of having departed from Aristotle's teaching in *De Anima* that the material or possible intellect is a power of the soul – a thesis which as we have just seen, Averroes concedes. However, he was trying to give this intellect a

---

28. *Averrois Cordubensis Commentarium Magnum* III, 17, pp. 436 f.
29. *Ibid.*, III, 5, p. 401.

universal, and to some extent transcendent status, which Aristotle probably did not envisage.[30] Nevertheless, on the status of the Active Intellect, the Philosopher and the Commentator were probably in agreement. As Aristotle has put it in *De Anima* III, 430a17, "Mind in this sense [that is, as active reason] is separable (*choristos*), impassible (*apathis*), unmixed (*amigis*), since it is in its essential nature activity." As understood by Averroes, those words meant that the Active Intellect was immaterial, independent of the conditions of change or passivity and fully actual. In addition, it was separable (*choristos*), in the sense that it was transcendent and universal. On the last point, Aristotle was far from being explicit, and this is what gave rise to the endless controversies among his commentators starting with Alexander of Aphrodisias in the second century C.E. Averroes was probably torn between the Avicennian concept of a transcendent Active Intellect and a more immanent interpretation of Aristotle's obscure texts.

30. For further discussion, see Chapters 10 and 11.

7

God and the Creation of the World

God's Existence and His Attributes

In one of his major theological treatises, the *Exposition of the Methods of Proof (al-Kashf)*, Averroes deals systematically with the questions of God's existence, His attributes and His creation of the world, before turning to such questions as free will and predestination, prophethood and resurrection.

The book opens with a discussion of the existence of God, a question which was at the center of theological and philosophical discussions in Islam and was destined to become a pivotal issue in Western Scholastic circles in the thirteenth and fourteenth centuries. In fact, Latin Scholastic treatises, such as St. Thomas Aquinas' *Summa Theologica*, open with this very question, preceded sometimes with the question of the justifiability of theological enquiry.

The Literalists (*Hashwiyah*), he explains, assert that God's existence is known exclusively from Scripture or accredited report (*sam'*) and give their assent to it on the basis of faith. Reason has nothing to do with this knowledge, according to them.

The Ash'arites, whose methods are similar to the Mu'tazilites with respect to this question according to Averroes, have held, contrariwise, that God's existence is known through reason. Their best-known argument rests on two premises: 1) that the world is temporal or created in time (*ḥādith*), and 2) that this temporality is a corollary of the fact that bodies are composed of indivisible particles or atoms and accidents, which, like those bodies, are temporal or created in time. This argument, generally referred to as the proof of temporality (*dalīl al-ḥudūth*), or as the Latin Scholastics called it, the argument *a novitate mundi*, goes back to the philosopher al-Kindī and beyond him to John Philoponus, known in the Arabic sources as John the Grammarian (d. 568).

Averroes criticizes this argument on two grounds. First, it entails that the Maker (*Muḥdith*) of the world is either temporal or eternal. If the former, then He will need a prior maker and that maker a prior maker and so on *ad infinitum*. If this Maker is said to be eternal, then his action in producing the created world would be eternal. The Mutakallimun, whether Mu'tazilite or Ash'arite, however, will not grant that the temporally created world is produced by a temporal agent, although one of their premises is that what is associated with the temporal is temporal. Nevertheless, to overcome this dilemma, they are forced to grant either that the world is eternal, which they deny, or that it is temporal, in which case its Maker is temporal (*ḥādith*), too, which they equally deny.

To counter these objections, Averroes explains, the Mutakallimun have resorted to a well-known expedient; namely, that the temporal world came into being through an eternal act of willing on the part of the Maker. This argument, however, fails, according to Averroes, to recognize that willing and doing or making, as applied to God, are entirely distinct; so that if we suppose the world to be created in time, then the action giving rise to this world would be in time. It is indifferent in this regard whether the will determining that action is temporal or eternal, prior to the action or simultaneous with it. In short, God's will is the precondition of His action in creating the world and is not the same as that action, of which the world is an instant product. Thus, there can be no interval between God's creating of the world and its coming-to-be, unless we assume that He was impotent or was deterred by some impediment, which is absurd.[1]

As for the second premise, or atomic composition of bodies, it is an abstruse question, "which the experts in the art of dialectic, let alone the

---

1. *Al-Kashf*, p. 136. Cf. *Tahāfut al-Tahāfut*, p. 150.

general public cannot fathom."[2] For this atomic composition is not a self-evident proposition and opinions regarding it are diametrically opposed to each other. The Ash'arite arguments in its support are mostly rhetorical and stem from confusing discrete and continuous quantities. The former, such as number, are reducible to indivisible parts, such as the unit, but the latter are not, in so far as every part thereof is divisible *ad infinitum*.

The same is true of the accidents, which the Mutakallimun held, subsist in the atoms. Here they reason by analogy from perceptible accidents to imperceptible, such as the heavenly spheres, which are not known to come to be in time, like perceptible accidents. For, neither the time nor the place of the universe, including the spheres, can be conceived as temporal or finite, since every event therein may be conceived as preceded by another event and every place contained in another place and so on *ad infinitum*.[3]

The second major argument for the existence of God, developed by a leading Ash'arite theologian, al-Juwayni (d. 1086), teacher of al-Ghazālī, is the argument from contingency, ultimately affiliated to Avicenna. According to this argument, whatever exists in the world could have been otherwise than it is, larger or smaller, higher or lower, more or less; and being contingent it must be temporal. For Averroes, the whole concept of contingency, on which this argument rests, is purely rhetorical and flies in the face of the evidence of our senses. It also impugns the wisdom of the Creator. For, whoever imagines that things, either as a whole or in part, could have been otherwise than the Creator has determined is really questioning His wisdom, for this wisdom necessarily entails that created entities are causally ordered and accordingly could not be otherwise. "For wisdom," Averroes writes in the *Incoherence (Tahāfut)*, "is nothing more than the knowledge of the causes of things. If things did not have any necessary causes determining their existence in the manner in which they are what they are, then there would really be no knowledge proper to the Wise Creator or anyone else."[4]

2. *Al-Kashf*, p. 135
3. *Ibid.*, pp. 140 f.
4. *Tahāfut al-Tahāfut*, p. 145.

It follows, therefore, that neither the argument from temporality nor the argument from contingency is a sound argument for the existence of God. What is the argument, Averroes then asks, which is accordant with the 'religious method' and which the Precious Book (i.e. the Qur'an) has recommended? This argument, he answers, is the twofold argument from providence and from invention.

The argument from providence rests on the premise that everything which exists in the world has come to be in a manner which accords with the welfare of mankind and is the product of the action of a Willful Agent. It cannot be the product of chance, as appears conclusively from observing the succession of day and night, the four seasons, the rivers and the seas and even man's location on earth, all of which are subservient to the welfare of mankind.

The argument from invention rests, on the other hand, on two premises which are ingrained in human nature. The first, which is self-evident, states that all existing entities are 'invented' by God, as the Qur'an states in verse 22:72: "Surely those whom you call upon, besides God, will never create a fly, even if they band together." The second is that every invented thing must have an Inventor, of whose invention many signs are observable in the world. Now, whoever wishes to know God as He really is must, therefore, investigate the nature of things, so as to grasp the real invention at the heart of things. "For whoever does not know the reality of a given thing will not understand the reality of (its) invention," as confirmed by the Qur'an itself, which states in verse 7:184 "Have they not considered the kingdom of the heavens and the earth and all the things God has created?" What is more, whoever investigates the wisdom underlying the creation of any given entity, the causes determining it and the purpose for which it was invented, will have a firmer grasp of the preceding proof of providence.

It is obvious from this analysis that Averroes is proposing to replace the two versions of the cosmological argument favored by the Mutakallimun by a version of the teleological argument, having a basis in the Qur'an. This is confirmed by the way in which, as we have just seen, he believes the argument from invention is a variation on the argument from providence. This is further confirmed by his definition of philosophy or wisdom in the opening part of the *Decisive Treatise (Faṣl al-Maqāl)* as "the investigation of existing entities or their consideration in so far as they manifest the Maker; I mean, in so far as they are made. For existing entities manifest the Maker to the extent that the art of making them is known; the more complete the knowledge of the art of making them, the more complete the knowledge of the Maker."[5] By contrast, it will be recalled, Aristotle had favored the cosmological argument, both in the *Physics* and the *Metaphysics*. In his lost sermon, *De Philosophia*, he had hinted at the teleological argument, although his general preference was clearly for the cosmological or etiological, which rested on the necessary causal connection between the world as effect and the First Principle or Cause. Surprisingly, Averroes does not exploit to the full in his theological writings this Aristotelian line of thinking, despite his insistence, especially in his polemic with al-Ghazālī in the *Incoherence of the Incoherence*, on the centrality of the causal principle in interpreting the concatenation of events or particulars in the world and the wisdom of their Maker.

With respect to the attributes of God, Averroes rejects al-Ghazālī's charge in the *Incoherence of the Philosophers* (*Tahāfut al-Falāsifah*) that the philosophers are negators of divine attributes (*mu'aṭṭilah*), like the Mu'tazilites, who rejected the Ash'arite thesis that God's attributes are distinct from His essence and insisted instead that these attributes are identical with that essence. They were charged later on by their critics, unjustly we believe, of stripping God of His attributes altogether.

In countering the charge of stripping God of His attributes, Averroes tends to go well beyond the Mu'tazilite position, which was on the whole in keeping with the view of Aristotle, who recognized no distinction in the First Principle between subject and predicate, essence and attribute. Be this as it may, Averroes argues, in rebutting al-Ghazālī's charges, that the philosophers do not actually deny the attributes of God, but insist that they are predicated of Him in a manner entirely different from that of the Mutakallimun. What the philosophers deny, he explains, is that the attributes of life, knowledge and power are predicated of God and of humans analogically, and maintain instead that they are predicated of

5. *Faṣl al-Maqāl*, p. 27.

Him by way of transcendence (*tanzīh*). Thus knowledge is predicated of
Him by virtue of the marvelous order we observe in the creation and the
way some creatures are subordinated to others. However, the philosophers
hold that the relation of this knowledge to particulars is unknown, and is,
in fact, *sui generis*, since it is radically different from our knowledge. It is,
as we have seen earlier, the *cause* of particulars, whereas our knowledge is
the *effect* of particulars. Beyond this, we are not able to assert positively
whether this knowledge is eternal or temporal; its modality (*kayfiyah*), like
that of His will, is entirely unknown or unknowable.[6]

The other attributes of life, will and power are predicable of God in a
way entirely different from man; life as a precondition of knowledge, will
as His prerogative in willing an object or its opposite and finally power as
His ability to bring the willed object into being.

Of the other attributes round which controversy raged in theological
and philosophical circles in the ninth century and beyond, it was speech
which gave rise to the most acrimonious exchanges and set the
Mu'tazilites and the Ash'arites at loggerheads. The former, whose cause
was championed by the Abbasid caliph al-Ma'mūn (813–833), held that
God's speech (*kalām*) embodied in the Qur'an was created, while the
Hanbalites challenged this view and insisted that the Qur'an was the
eternal and uncreated speech of God – a proposition in which the
Ash'arites and the traditionalists concurred. In dealing with this knotty
issue, Averroes exhibits great dialectical skill. The Qur'an, he argues, is
God's eternal speech (*kalām*), as the Ash'arites and the Hanbalites held,
but the *words* which express this speech are created by God, in one sense,
and are our own doing (*fi'l*), in another. Here Averroes distinguishes
between words we use in ordinary speech and those we use in reciting the
Qur'an. The former are of our doing, the latter are God's creation.
However, the letters (*ḥuruf*) in which the Qur'an is written are of our
doing, 'by God's leave.' They should be glorified, "because they denote the
words created by God and the meaning which is uncreated."[7] Thus,
"whoever considers the words, apart from the meaning, without
distinction, will say that the Qur'an is created; while whoever considers

6. *Tahāfut al-Tahāfut*, p. 149.
7. *Al-Kashf*, p. 164.

the meaning which the words denote will say it is uncreated."[8] The truth
is that the two views should be combined. He then comments that the root
of the difficulty is that the Ash'arites denied that God is the author of
speech, since this would render Him a bearer of the accident of speech,
asserting instead that speech is an eternal attribute subsisting in God, like
knowledge, power and life. The Mu'tazilites, on the other hand, held that
speech is the work of the speaker and is tantamount to the utterance (*lafz*)
only. That is why they asserted that the Qur'an is created; since it is not
necessary that speech should subsist in the speaker, as the Ash'arites held.

For Averroes, the latter claim is valid where human speakers are
concerned, both as regards the 'soul's (inner) speech' and the words
denoting it; but with respect to the Creator, the inner "speech of the soul
is what subsists in Him; but that which denotes it does not subsist in
Him."[9] The real difference between the Ash'arites and the Mu'tazilites,
according to Averroes, consists precisely in the claim of the former that
speech, as an accident, must subsist in the speaker, and for this reason they
denied that God is the author of speech, since this would render Him a
bearer of accidents. The Mu'tazilites, on the other hand, having identified
speech with the action of the speaker, were led to identify it with the
utterances only and concluded, accordingly, that the Qur'an is created.
Utterance, in so far as it is an action of the speaker, does not have to
subsist in the speaker, as the Ash'arites claimed. The latter claim, Averroes
concludes, is true of human speakers, where both the inner speech of the
soul and the words denoting it are concerned; but in the case of God, the
speech of the soul subsists in Him, but that which denotes it does not
subsist in Him, as already mentioned. What Averroes is trying to assert is
that the meanings of the Qur'anic verses are eternal or uncreated, but the
words in which they are expressed or the letters in which they are written
are created in time – a conciliatory position which the Hanbalites were
not willing to concede.

With respect to the two attributes of hearing and sight, Averroes is
explicit that they, too, belong to God, in so far as His knowledge embraces
all cognitions, rational or other, on the one hand, and in so far as He is the

8. *Ibid.*, p. 164.
9. *Ibid.*, p. 164.

Creator of the objects of hearing and sight, and accordingly is conversant with them, on the other. This, he states without much ado, is "the measure of knowledge [pertaining to this subject] that Scripture has explicitly called for, as far as the general public is concerned."[10]

Averroes next tackles the equally knotty question of the attributes in relation to God, rejecting both the Ash'arite view that they are distinct from His essence and that of the Mu'tazilites who identified essence and attribute in God. He finds a parallel between the Ash'arite view and the Christian Trinity, since the Ash'arites are forced to grant, either that the essence subsists in itself while the attributes subsist in it, or each one of these attributes subsists in itself, as the Christian Trinity implies.[11] The identity of essence and attribute upheld by the Mu'tazilites is gratuitous, he goes on to assert, since it is self-evident that the knower is other than the knowledge attributed to him and the same goes for the other attributes. This view, at any rate, is apt to lead the general public astray and is, according to Averroes, an innovation (*bid'ah*).[12]

Divine Justice and Knowledge

Another issue which set the Ash'arites and the Mu'tazilites at loggerheads was divine justice, with which Averroes deals in the *Exposition*, in the context of God's actions. He begins by criticizing the Ash'arites for having taken a position on this question that is contrary to both reason and Scripture. According to this position, actions are just or unjust by virtue of the prescriptions of the divine law (*Shari'ah*), or as the early Ash'arites had put it, by virtue of what God commands or prohibits. Apart from the fact that this view entails that nothing is just or unjust in itself, it renders this concept entirely meaningless in the case of God, who is the First Lawgiver. In addition, it allows that the most grievous sins, such as blasphemy or polytheism (*shirk*), would have been just had the divine law prescribed them.

10. *Ibid.*, p. 165.
11. *Ibid.*, p. 166.
12. *Ibid.*, p. 166.

That this position is contrary to Scripture (*shar'*) can be ascertained by a perusal of the Qur'an, which asserts in a variety of places that God is not unjust, as in verse 3:16, which states: "God bears witness that there is no god but He, and so do the angels and men of learning. He upholds justice," and verse 10:45, which states: "Surely God does not wrong people at all, but people wrong themselves," and finally verse 41:45, which states: "Your Lord is not unjust to the servants."

As for those Qur'anic verses which speak of God as guiding whomever He pleases and leading astray whomever He pleases (Qur'an 16:95 and 74:34), they are, Averroes argues, inconclusive; for, they are contradicted by other verses in which God is said, as already mentioned, not to be unjust to His servants and one who "does not approve of disbelief in His servants" (verse 39:9), and accordingly cannot be said to lead them astray. The solution of this problem, according to Averroes, is to recognize that the references to guiding mankind or leading them astray are to be understood as referring to "the prior will [of God] which determined that the varieties of existing entities shall include creatures who are astray; I mean, disposed by their natures to being misled and driven to error by the causes inducing them to error, from outside or inside."[13]

The justification of this divine disposition, according to Averroes, is that it was ordained by divine wisdom that there shall exist among mankind some people who are by nature evil, but are a minority, and those who are good, who are the majority. Therefore, as ordained by divine wisdom, the two choices open to God were either: "Not to create those species which are liable to evil for the least part, or good for the most part, in which case the greater good would not have come to be, on account of the lesser evil; or to create those species, wherein the greater good exists side by side with the lesser evil."[14] It is self-evident, argues Averroes, that the coexistence of the greater good with the lesser evil is preferable to the non-existence of the greater good, on account of the possible existence of the lesser evil. In the last analysis, the real justification of God's action is that "He is the Creator of good for the sake of the good, and of evil for the sake of the good; I mean, on account of the

13. *Ibid.*, pp. 235 f.
14. *Ibid.*, pp. 236 f.

good attendant on it."[15] It follows that God's creation of evil is just. For instance, the creation of fire is just, on account of the fact that it is essential for the subsistence of those entities which cannot subsist without fire. However, fire could accidentally cause the burning of some valuable object which we did not wish to burn. Nevertheless, compared to the good resulting from fire, the evil that could ensue upon its existence is comparatively smaller, and consequently its existence is preferable to its non-existence.

A key argument of the Ash'arites is that God, as the Lord of Lords, is not answerable for His actions, and thus cannot be described as just or unjust, in support of which they quote the Qur'anic verse: "He is not questioned about what He does, but they [meaning mankind] are questioned" (21:23). For Averroes, this and similar verses should be understood to mean that God is under no obligation to perform a certain action or its opposite, owing to the fact that He is in no need of that action or its consequences. For the fulfillment of such need may be essential for a finite agent in so far as it contributes to his perfection. Now, the Creator transcends these conditions to which mankind is subject. For mankind acts justly in order to derive some advantage or other from such action. God, however, acts justly because the perfection which belongs to Him essentially entails that He shall always act justly.[16]

Having examined the way in which the various attributes are predicated of God by the two rival factions of Mu'tazilite and Ash'arite Mutakallimun, Averroes turns to another major point of controversy between them; namely, whether these attributes are distinct from the divine essence, as the Ash'arites held, or identical with it, as the Mu'tazilites did. For him, the whole controversy is entirely misguided. "The public," he writes, "should only know what Scripture has stated explicitly; namely, that [these attributes] exist without any further questions. For it is impossible for the public to achieve certainty in that regard."[17]

As for the philosophers, he continues, in so far as "they seek the knowledge of existing entities through reason, without relying on the

15. *Ibid.*, p. 238.
16. *Ibid.*, p. 138.
17. *Ibid.*, p. 167.

words of him who exhorts them to accept it without proof,"[18] they have been able to draw certain conclusions from observing sensible entities in the world of generation and corruption. Thus they found that they are made up of matter and form, are animate or inanimate and manifest a certain order and harmony, which could not be entirely fortuitous. In their search for a first cause of such generable and corruptible entities, they reasoned that it is either a heavenly body or an immaterial substance. Eventually, they reached the conclusion that this order and harmony should be referred to a single Reason, who is the First Principle of all things and is entirely immaterial. He apprehends Himself only, and by virtue of this apprehension, "apprehends all existing entities in the best way, and according to the best order and the best harmony."[19] Contrary to Aristotle's argument in *Metaphysics* XII, 1074b25, that this First Principle, in His transcendence and perfection, can only partake of the knowledge of the noblest objects in the best way possible and cannot for that reason apprehend anything beneath Himself, Averroes re-asserts the Qur'anic concept of divine omniscience.

A characteristic feature of the First's knowledge of Himself is that in the act of knowing Himself the object and the subject are identified and thus He may be described as thought thinking thought, or as al-Fārābī and Avicenna have put it, *'aql wa 'āqil wa ma'qūl.*

The mode of this knowledge, Averroes then explains, is neither particular nor universal – a question over which controversy raged in theological and philosophical circles; it is entirely *sui generis.* It cannot be universal as Avicenna had proposed, because universal knowledge is potential and God is entirely free of potentiality; nor particular because particulars are infinite and therefore cannot be fully circumscribed. As we have seen in his response to al-Ghazālī, God's knowledge, for Averroes, is the *cause* of the thing known, whereas our knowledge is the *effect.* It follows that "in so far as He knows Himself only, He knows all those entities of whose existence He is the cause . . . The Almighty is He who absolutely knows the nature of the existent, qua existent, which is Himself. Therefore knowledge is predicated of Him and of ourselves

---

18. *Tahāfut al-Tahāfut*, p. 210.
19. *Ibid.*, p. 214. Cf. *Tafsīr* III, pp. 1632 f.

equivocally. For His knowledge is the cause of the existent and the existent is the cause of our knowledge,"[20] as already mentioned.

Having described the First Principle as thought thinking itself, Averroes proceeds to argue that, as such, it must partake of the greatest pleasure, since the essence of pleasure is thought. To pleasure should be added life, for the actuality of thought is life, as Aristotle had put it in *Metaphysics* XII.

Continuous versus Discontinuous Creation

Next Averroes proceeds to discuss the two primary actions of the First Principle or God; namely, the creation of the world and the commissioning of prophets. As regards the creation of the world, he begins by countering al-Ghazālī's charge in the *Incoherence of the Philosophers* (Question III) that, in so far as they regard the world as eternal, the philosophers are guilty of dissimulation (*talbīs*) when they refer to God as the Creator of the world. For such a world, having existed since all time, does not require a Creator, according to him. When the philosophers speak of God as the Maker or Creator of the world they are at best speaking figuratively or metaphorically.

For Averroes this charge rests on a misunderstanding of the nature of action or making, as predicated of God. The philosophers in fact distinguish between two modes of action in the visible world, natural and voluntary, neither of which applies to God, according to them; the former because it involves necessitation or compulsion, the latter because it involves some want or desire, of which God is free. Thus, the philosophers do not deny that God is capable of action; they simply deny that those two modes of action are predicable of Him. Their view is that the world arises by virtue of God's knowledge and will. "However, the *manner* in which God has made [the world] and wills it is not clear in this context, since there is no parallel to His will in the visible world, ... and just as the modality of His knowledge is not known, so is the modality of His will."[21] Notwithstanding, Averroes is willing to concede that God is said by the philosophers to be the Creator or

20. *Tafsīr* III, pp. 1707 f.
21. *Tahāfut al-Tahāfut*, p. 149.

Producer of the universe, which is eternal, in the sense that it is in 'continuous production' and goes on to argue that, of the two modes of production (*ihdāth*), the continuous (*dā'im*) and the discontinuous (*muqati'*), the former is more appropriately predicated of God than the latter.[22]

It follows that there is nothing in the philosophers' assertion that the world is eternal to suggest that it could have dispensed with a Maker or Creator, who is God. For the series of causes which have given rise to the totality of entities and events we refer to collectively as the world can be shown to terminate in a First Cause, who is the First Principle of motion or becoming in the world, to whom all the forms of generation and corruption must be referred, according to the philosophers. By denying the necessary correlation of cause and effect in the world, the Ash'arites have surrendered the world to the vagaries of randomness (*ittifāq*). In that case, they are forced to admit, like the advocates of chance, by whom Averroes no doubt means Democritus and his Materialist followers, "that there is no Maker [of the world] and that everything which takes place in this world is due to material causes only."[23]

In the *Large Commentary on the Metaphysics*, Averroes reviews the various views of creation or origination (*ījād*) of existing entities, which he reduces to four.

1. The view of the advocates of latency or immanence (*kumūn*), who contend that everything is latent in everything else, production being simply the way in which the properties or forms latent or immanent in the object become manifest. The agent, on this view, is simply the mover who effects this manifestation. Averroes does not name any advocates of this view.

2. The antithesis of this view is that of invention and origination (*ibdā'*), which stipulates that the agent brings the entity in its entirety into being, without any need for a matter on which it operates. "This is the generally accepted view of the theologians of our religion and that of the Christians."[24]

---

22. *Ibid.*, p. 162.
23. *Al-Kashf*, p. 200.
24. *Tafsīr* III, p. 1497.

3. The view of Avicenna, who held that the agent simply generates or produces the form and causes it to subsist in matter and for this reason is referred to as 'the giver of forms.'[25] A variation on this view is attributed to Themistius and al-Fārābī, who held that the agent in question is either material or immaterial.

4. "The view which we have received from Aristotle . . . whose view we have found the least open to doubt and the most accordant with reality . . . and the farthest removed from contradiction."[26] According to this view, the agent simply causes the compounds·of form and matter to come into being, by moving matter or causing it to pass from potentiality to actuality.

The chief merit of this view, according to Averroes, is that the agent or maker does not invent the forms, or else something would have come into being from nothing, which is absurd. It was for this reason that Aristotle believed that the form is not generated or corrupted except accidentally; namely, in relation to the generation or corruption of the compound of which it forms the active ingredient, as compared with matter which forms the passive ingredient.

Here Averroes launches a violent attack against the theologians of "the three religious communities (*milal*) existing today," meaning no doubt Muslims, Christians and Jews, for adhering to the view that things, as indeed the whole world, can come to be out of nothing by way of invention. He then singles 'the Mutakallimun of our religion' for special reprobation. For when they did not discover in the world here below an agent who acts by way of invention and origination (*ibdā'*), they proceeded to posit a Single Agent of this type, who produces all things directly and without any intermediary. They held in addition that the actions of this Agent can take contrary forms at the same time, denying thereby that fire burns or water quenches the thirst, on the arbitrary ground that natural agents are incapable of production or invention, which is the exclusive prerogative of the Unique Agent in question.[27]

---

25. *Kitāb al-Najāt*, p. 319.
26. *Tafsīr* III, p. 1497.
27. *Ibid.*, pp. 1503 f.

In responding to al-Ghazālī's charge that, when the philosophers speak of God as the Cause of the world or its Agent, they are speaking figuratively and should for that reason be declared godless, Averroes reasserts the Aristotelian concept of causal efficacy, as the antithesis of the above-mentioned concept of the inertness of natural bodies. The concept of making or production is tantamount in the last analysis to the act of bringing together (*ribāt, tarkīb*) matter and form. It follows that God as the Supreme Agent who brings together the matter and form of the universe is the Maker of the universe. He is, in addition, the Preserver of things in the most perfect manner. Moreover, unlike other, finite agents, God's action emanates from His all-encompassing knowledge and His absolute generosity and goodness, wherein He is entirely free from any determination or constraint. For this reason, Averroes concludes, the philosophers believe that as the "Cause of continuous production (*ihdāth dā'im*), God is more worthy of the name of Producer than any one who is the cause of discontinuous production (*ihdāth munqaṭi'*),"[28] or creation in time, as already mentioned.

It will be noted at this point that Averroes has successfully rebutted al-Ghazālī's charge of godlessness or irreligion leveled at the philosophers, and reaffirmed God's prerogative as the Maker and Preserver of the world. On the question of the eternity of the universe, he has remained adamant in adhering to the Aristotelian thesis of an eternal universe, of which he believed that God is, nonetheless, the Supreme Maker or Creator. In that respect, he has clearly gone beyond Aristotle, who nowhere in his extant works has attributed to God or the Unmoved Mover a creative or generative function. In *Metaphysics* XII, 1072b16, it is true, he declares that "on such a principle [i.e. God], then depend the heavens and the world of nature." Such dependence, however, is not invested with any generative or creative meaning. Rather, the contrary. In commenting on God's mode of self-knowing, he is anxious to relieve Him of the burden of knowing or communicating with a universe which does not rise to the rank of the 'most divine and precious' (*Met.* XII. 1074b27), i.e. Himself.

28. *Tahāfut al-Tahāfut*, p. 162.

Nonetheless, Averroes stops short of explicitly espousing the Qur'anic thesis of creation *ex nihilo*, which the generality of the Mutakallimun, almost without exception, adhered to. Some of the philosophers, with al-Kindī at their head, even defended this thesis with strict philosophical arguments. Only in one puzzling passage in the *Decisive Treatise (al-Faṣl)* does Averroes speak of creation *ex nihilo* with some ambiguity. Here he divides existing entities into three categories:

1. Observable particulars of sense, such as animals and plants, which have come into being by some agent and from something; namely, some material substratum. Both the philosophers and the Ash'arites, he comments, are in agreement that these entities have come to be out of something and were preceded by time.

2. The opposite of this category is a Being who has not come into existence out of something or from some agent, and has not been preceded by time. This Being, according to all the parties mentioned above, is eternal and is known through demonstration; "He is God Almighty, the Maker of all things and their Preserver in being."[29]

3. The third category of existing entities is intermediate between the two. "It is an entity which has not come to be out of something or was preceded by time, but exists through the action of an Agent. This is the world as a whole."[30]

Notwithstanding, Averroes has not explained anywhere how the third category, or the world as a whole, has come into being out of nothing and was not preceded by time, unlike everything else made of matter and form. The only possible explanation is that the world has come into being from Prime Matter, which for Aristotle is not, qua Prime Matter, anything at all. For Plato, this matter is identified more explicitly in the *Timaeus* with nothing (*to me on*). It follows that the world as a whole may be said, in a sense, to have come into being out of nothing. In his desire to appease the Mutakallimun and to substantiate his claim that religion (i.e. Islam) is in perfect harmony with philosophy, Averroes may be said to have predicated the concept of production or origination (*ihdāth*, *ījād*) of God,

29. *Faṣl al-Maqāl*, p. 41.
30. *Ibid.*, p. 41.

without abandoning the concept of the eternity of the world. The latter concept is thoroughly Aristotelian, but the former, as we have just mentioned, is not. As W. D. Ross has put it: "God, as conceived by Aristotle, has a knowledge which is not a knowledge of the universe, and an influence on the universe, which does not flow from this knowledge . . . For him, that God should know Himself, and that He should know other things, are alternatives, and in affirming the first alternative, he implicitly denies the second."[31] On the critical issue of creation, Ross is even more explicit, "If the question be asked, whether Aristotle thinks of God as Creator of the universe, the answer must certainly be that he does not,"[32] adding that Aristotle expressly argues in *De Coelo* 301b31 and 279b12f. against the creation of the universe.

This, then, is a question on which Averroes has clearly departed from the teaching of the Master, for whom he had the highest regard. His motives must, therefore, be interpreted as theological; namely the desire to bring philosophy into harmony with religion. On the whole, it is fair to say that he achieved his goal skillfully, and although he did not succeed fully in appeasing the Mutakallimun, he has demonstrated a philosophical acumen which was almost unequaled, by reconciling the two concepts of eternity and creation, deemed by those Mutakallimun to be irreconcilable. The clue to this reconciliation was his concept of 'continuous origination' (*ihdāth dā'im*) or eternal creation, as already mentioned.

Prophets as Lawgivers

In addition to 'continuous creation,' known in Medieval circles as *creatio ab aeterno*, Averroes ascribes to God, in perfect consonance with official Islamic teaching, the prerogative of commissioning prophets or divine messengers to mankind. He begins by discussing the view of the Mutakallimun that God, as a free and omnipotent Agent, is at liberty to send messengers to mankind, just as any human master may send messengers to his own subordinates. As evidence of the veracity of their claims to be God's genuine messengers, those messengers have been

31. *Aristotle*, p. 183.
32. *Ibid.*, p. 184.

God and the Creation of the World 91

empowered to perform certain extraordinary deeds, known as miracles. In that way, the Mutakallimun have sought to answer the Brahmins, who reject the whole concept of prophethood or revelation, as do most naturalists and atheists.

For Averroes, the validity of the second argument, or the probative force of miracles, is purely rhetorical and is suited for the general public only. It depends on two major premises: 1) that, indeed, whoever performs a miracle is a messenger of God; and 2) such miracles are possible only at the hands of such a messenger. These two propositions, he argues, are indicative statements whose truth or validity cannot be ascertained either by recourse to reason or to revelation. In the latter case, it is because the validity of revelation itself must be ascertained first, or else we would be involved in a petition of principle or circular reasoning. In the former case, it is because reason itself cannot affirm or deny, on its own, the possibility of divine missions to mankind at the hands of so-called prophets or divine messengers. In order to prove the validity of the claims of such a messenger, we must first prove that miracle is the *sine qua non* of divine missions. "The miraculous," he writes, "does not prove a [prophetic] mission, because reason does not see any connection between the two."[33] In fact, he adds, the Prophet (Muḥammad) himself "did not call on any individual or nation to believe in his mission or what he was bringing forth, by offering, in advance of his claims, a miraculous deed, such as turning one object into another."[34] All the prophetic favors and miracles, associated with his prophetic mission, appeared during his ministry, without being attended by a challenge. This is confirmed by the Qur'an itself, which states (verse 17:92), in the mouth of pagans; "We will not believe you until you cause a spring to gush out from the ground for us," followed by the response: "Say, glory to my Lord, am I anything other than a human messenger" (17:96). The only miracle the Prophet presented mankind with is the 'Precious Book,' i.e. the Qur'an.

Here the question may arise, Averroes continues: "But how does the Precious Book, as a miracle, prove the claim of the Prophet to be a genuine divine messenger?" For the probative force of miracle, in

33. *Al-Kashf,* p. 212.
34. *Ibid.,* p. 213.

confirming a prophetic mission, is as much in question as the claim of a specific person (i.e. Muḥammad) that he is indeed its bearer. The matter is further complicated by the fact that opinion is divided, regarding the specific way in which the Qur'an, as divine speech (*kalām*), is to be viewed as miraculous or inimitable. Some scholars have argued that it is divine speech in itself, others that it is miraculous by virtue of 'deterrence' (*ṣarf*), or the way in which mankind has been deterred by God from attempting to imitate it. Our response, states Averroes, is that the Qur'an confirms the Prophet's claim to be God's messenger in two ways. The first, or general way, is that the existence of prophets or divine messengers is self-evident; the second is that the function of this class of people, known as prophets, is to promulgate laws for mankind, through divine inspiration, rather than human instruction. The existence of such a class of people can only be denied by one who is willing to deny attested reports, such as the existence of various species of creatures one has not observed, or that of certain individuals pre-eminent in wisdom. It should be understood that the truth of such existence is a matter of historical record, which, if sufficiently corroborated, cannot be denied by a reasonable person. This is a matter, he adds, in which philosophers and the bulk of mankind, with the exception of the Materialists (*Dahriyah*) concur; namely, "that there exists in fact a class of people who receive revelation [from God], intended to communicate to mankind certain forms of knowledge and virtuous actions, which are conducive to their well-being, while deterring them from partaking of certain false beliefs and vicious actions. This, in fact, is the function of the prophets."[35]

In the *Incoherence* (*Tahāfut*), Averroes has developed more forcefully the thesis that divinely ordained laws are essential for man's well-being, "in so far as they are the necessary preconditions of man's acquisition of moral and theoretical virtues, as well as the practical arts."[36] The reason is that man's life in this world is not possible without the practical arts; while in this world and the next, it is not possible without the theoretical virtues. Moreover, neither the practical arts nor the theoretical virtues are possible without the moral virtues, which cannot become ingrained in the

35. *Ibid.*, p. 215.
36. *Tahāfut al-Tahāfut*, p. 580.

soul without the knowledge of God and glorifying Him by means of certain ritual observances.[37] Averroes further explains that religious laws (*sharā'i'*) themselves can be shown to be equivalent to those fundamental 'civil arts,' whose principles are derived from both reason and revelation, especially that part thereof which is common to the various accredited religions.

Moreover, it is generally accepted that the fundamental principles of religious belief, such as whether God exists or not, whether He ought to be worshiped or not, and whether eternal bliss in the hereafter is possible or not, should not be questioned. For we find that the various religions, of which Averroes mentions Islam, Christianity, Judaism and the Sabaean religion, (mentioned in the Qur'an), concur in affirming the truth of God's existence, His attributes and the reality of life after death, although they differ with respect to the degree or manner of such affirmation. The reason for this difference is that, "in so far as they aim at wisdom by recourse to a method accessible to all men, [those religions] are deemed to be necessary by [the philosophers]."[38] However, the philosophers recognize that, whereas philosophy aims at determining the happiness of those people who are able to acquire wisdom by recourse to reason, religion aims at teaching the general public by recourse to other methods of discourse. These include the dialectical method suited to the Mutakallimun and the rhetorical, suited to the general public. Nevertheless, none of those religions have overlooked drawing attention to what is proper to the one class rather than the other, so as to ensure the felicity of each. In addition, they have prescribed that a person should choose the best religion available to him, Averroes writes, "even though all [religions] are deemed by him as true." One should understand, however, that the best is eventually 'abrogated' by what is better. That is why, he explains, the Alexandrian philosophers adopted Islam when they learnt about it, just as the philosophers who lived in Byzantium adopted Christianity when it reached them. Moreover, there is no doubt that there were many philosophers among the Children of Israel, as can be seen from the books attributed to Solomon (i.e. the so-called Books of Wisdom). In fact,

37. *Ibid.*, p. 581.
38. *Ibid.*, p. 583.

Averroes concludes, "philosophy has always existed among the adepts of revelation, i.e. the prophets, peace be on them. Thus, the soundest proposition [in this regard] is that every prophet is a philosopher (*ḥakīm*), but not every philosopher is a prophet."[39] It is for this reason that men of learning (*'ulamā*) have been described as the heirs of the prophets.

This, he continues, is the general consensus of the philosophers who insist that the practical principles and laws laid down in every religion should be received gratefully from the prophets and other lawgivers. This is particularly true of those laws which exhort mankind to virtuous conduct, performing prayers, and other observances prescribed in that religion.

Superiority of Islamic Law

As for the other principle which confirms the prophethood of Muḥammad, according to Averroes, it consists in the maxim that whoever is found to lay down laws by divine inspiration is a genuine prophet. Now, this principle is indubitable, as far as human nature is concerned. For it is self-evident that, for example, the function of the physician is to heal the sick and that of the prophet is to promulgate divinely ordained laws. It follows that whoever is found to heal the sick will be recognized as a physician, and by analogy, whoever is found to promulgate divine laws will be recognized as a prophet.

Averroes then advances a series of arguments to support his thesis that divinely ordained laws are indispensable for attaining a life of virtue in this world and happiness in the world-to-come, and that those laws "cannot be learnt by means of human instruction, art or philosophy," but revelation only.

Having laid this down as a general maxim or major premise, Averroes goes on to argue that, in so far as these laws are embodied in the Precious Book (Qur'an) in the most perfect manner, it follows that that Book is divinely revealed. This is confirmed by the fact that the Prophet Muḥammad, as the recipient of that revelation, was illiterate and grew up in the midst of "a vulgar and bedouin nation." The members of that nation

39. *Ibid.*, p. 583.

never practiced any sciences or were credited with any investigative skills, unlike the Greeks and other nations by whom philosophy or wisdom was consummated over the centuries.[40]

Moreover, if we examine the laws laid down in the Precious Book for the purpose of ensuring a life of virtue in this world and happiness in the world-to-come, in comparison with the laws embodied in other Scriptures, we will find that "they excel all other laws in this respect to an infinite degree."[41] Hence, if the laws laid down in the Old and New Testaments, which cannot be presumed to have been completely altered or corrupted (as the Islamic tradition presupposes), are examined, "the superiority of the laws laid down for us, Muslims, as compared with the laws laid down for Jews and Christians" is found to be unquestioned.[42]

As evidence of the universal character of the laws embodied in the Qur'an and intended to secure the happiness of all mankind, Averroes quotes the words of the Prophet, who is reported to have said: "I have been sent to the red and black [nations]," meaning all mankind, and the Qur'anic verse, 7:157: "Say, O people, I am God's messenger to you all." From this, Averroes infers that the evidence of Muḥammad's prophethood and the miraculousness of the Qur'an are unique. It differs from the evidence found in the Old or New Testament, such as Moses turning the stick into a serpent or Jesus raising the dead or healing the blind and the leper; since they are not necessarily indicative of the property whereby a prophet is a prophet. They are rather extrinsic (*barrāni*), whereas the evidence of the Qur'an is intrinsic or of 'the appropriate and pertinent type,' which confirms the Prophet's claim to be a prophet in the same way healing confirms the claim of the physician to be a physician. Moreover, the miraculousness of the Qur'an is apt, for this reason, to convince the general public and men of learning alike; whereas the other kinds of miracles are apt to convince the general public only. Averroes is content to make this assertion without any further arguments of the type urged by commentators or religious scholars in support of the inimitability (*i'jāz*) of the Qur'an, whether on literary or substantive grounds. He appears to

40. *Al-Kashf*, p. 219.
41. *Ibid.*, p. 219.
42. *Ibid.*, p. 220.

incline to the view that the Qur'an is miraculous by virtue of the legislation it embodies, since it is of the type that exceeds human capacity, let alone that of a person, i.e. Muḥammad, who was illiterate and, as already mentioned, grew up in a primitive, bedouin milieu.

8

Ethics and Politics

The Four Primary Virtues

We have already seen the role that religious laws play, for Averroes, in ensuring the life of virtue in this world and happiness, or eternal felicity, in the world-to-come. Ethical questions formed for this reason the core of some of his writings, including a summary of Aristotle's *Ethics*, which has not survived in Arabic, but of which Hebrew and Latin translations have survived. He has, in addition, written a middle commentary on the *Nicomachean Ethics*, of which two Latin translations by Hermann the German and Bernard Feliciano have survived.[1]

As far as politics is concerned, Averroes wrote a paraphrase (*jawāmi'*) of Plato's *Republic*, which has also survived only in Latin and Hebrew, but has been translated into English twice, by E. I. J. Rosenthal (1958) and Ralph Lerner (1974). In the Preface, Averroes refers to the close correlation between the two sciences of ethics and politics, embodied in Aristotle's *Nicomachean Ethics* and his *Politics*, which he says "has not fallen into our hands."[2] He does not appear to have been aware of the fact that the *Politics* was the only major work of Aristotle which, for some unknown reason, had not been translated into Arabic, a situation that was not remedied until modern times.

1. See *In Moralia Nicomachea Expositione.*
2. *Averroes on Plato's "Republic"*, p. 4.

Next, he observes that 'practical science,' with its two divisions, ethics
and politics, differs from the theoretical sciences in so far as its subject is
action, contrary to the theoretical sciences whose subject is only
knowledge. Ethics, however, has two subdivisions corresponding to the
two subdivisions of medicine, the hygienic and the therapeutic. The first
subdivision is concerned with the way in which the habits and volitional
activities, which form the subject-matter of ethics, are established in the
soul; the second with the way they are restored, once they are gone. It is
for this reason that it is shown in the first subdivision that human
perfections are of four kinds, theoretical virtues, cogitative (or reflective),
moral and technical, which appear to correspond to Aristotle's
classification in the *Nicomachean Ethics* (Book 6) of the intellectual virtues
into intuitive reason (*nous*), scientific knowledge (*episteme*), practical
wisdom (*phronesis*) and practical art (*techne*). All these virtues or
perfections, he adds, are for the sake of the theoretical and serve as a
preparation for them.

To achieve these virtues or perfections, it is not possible, Averroes
argues, for the individual to act independently of his fellow men; that is
why man is described (by Aristotle) as a political animal (*zoon politikon*).
Political association, however, is not only the precondition of human
perfection or virtue, but even of man's survival; since provision for his
everyday needs requires the assistance of his fellow-men, as Plato has
stated in the *Republic*. He then proceeds to draw a parallel between the
soul and the state, along essentially Platonic lines, and to enumerate the
virtues proper to each part thereof. Thus the soul, he says, is wise to the
extent its theoretical part rules the lower two parts; namely, the spirited
(*thymos*) and the appetitive. It is courageous by virtue of the spirited part
being subordinated to the theoretical, and temperate by virtue of the
appetitive part being subordinate to the theoretical, too. When all the
three parts of the soul are rationally ordered, justice arises. This virtue is
then defined as "nothing more than that every human in the city do the
work that is his by nature, in the best way he possibly can."[3] This is
possible only when all the parts of the city or that state are submissive to

3. *Ibid.*, p. 7. Cf. *Republic* IV, 431A.

what the theoretical sciences and those who possess them decree. By those who possess those theoretical sciences, he obviously meant the philosopher–king and his associates, i.e. the guardians, as Plato had called them in the *Republic.* Similarly, within the soul as the counterpart of the state, justice consists in "every one of its parts doing only what it has to do in the appropriate manner and at the appropriate time."[4] This is possible only when reason rules the other two parts, i.e. the spirited and the appetitive.

Justice and temperance, Averroes then explains, differ from the other two virtues in that they cut across the three parts of the city or the soul, unlike courage which is the specific virtue of the spirited part and wisdom which is the specific virtue of the rational part. With respect to temperance, Averroes appears to diverge from Plato's thesis that this virtue is indeed the specific virtue of the appetitive part of the soul and the working class in the state. For him it has a more comprehensive scope.

Be this as it may, Averroes tries, in his *Commentary on the Nicomachean Ethics,* to correlate the Platonic notion of justice, as the virtue which consists in the harmony within the soul and the state, and Aristotle's notion of universal or common justice. That virtue Aristotle had identified with perfect virtue, which is not confined to oneself, as Plato implied, but extends to our dealings with our neighbors. It is the mark of "the perfectly just man," Averroes writes, "to exercise his virtue in himself, as well as [in his dealings] with others."[5] As Aristotle has explained, universal justice is not part, but rather the whole of virtue, "because it is the actual exercise of complete virtue . . . and he who possesses it can exercise his virtue, not only in himself, but towards his neighbors also."[6]

Particular justice, which is the political counterpart of universal justice, admits of two subdivisions, distributive and rectificatory. The former consists in distributing money and honors equitably, the latter in restoring 'the proportion' disturbed by giving to equals unequally and to unequals equally which is the essence of injustice.[7]

4. *Ibid.,* p. 7. Cf *Republic* IV, 432c.
5. *In Moralia Nicomachea, Expositione,* fol. 65b.
6. *Nicomachean Ethics* V, 1129b 30.
7. *In Moralia Nicomachea, Expositione,* fol. 65b.

To complete the ethical enquiry, Averroes then raises three questions:

1. What are the conditions under which each of the virtues is best acquired; since the end of moral instruction, as Aristotle says, is to act, not just to know?

2. How may the virtues be established in the souls of the youth and made to grow with age and, conversely, how may the opposite vices be eradicated from their souls? Here Averroes notes that there is an analogy between the science of ethics and the art of medicine, in so far as the first part, or instilling the virtues in the soul, corresponds to hygiene, while the other part corresponds to therapy or the art of healing.

3. What habits or virtues are more likely to make the effect of each of the four virtues more complete, and which habits hinder the process of moral education and growth? This, however, cannot be understood unless the ends of these perfections, which we call virtues, are known, and, unless, at the political and social levels, the relations of the different parts or classes of the state are clearly defined.[8]

In so far as the subject-matter of ethics is volitional activity, it follows that the discussion of free will is central to the ethical enquiry. In the religious and political context in which the question of free will (*qadar*) was raised early in Muslim history, controversy turned, during the early Umayyad period, starting at the end of the seventh century, on the relation of free will and divine predestination (*qaḍā'*). The so-called Qadaris at Damascus and Basrah, such as Ma'bad al-Juhani (d. 699) and Ghaylān al-Dimashqi (d. 743), challenged the apparently official doctrine that all human actions are predestined by God, so that the actions of the caliphs, however cruel or repressive, cannot be questioned, since they form part of God's inexorable decree. The Umayyads naturally regarded that challenge as a threat to their authority, and accordingly dealt very harshly with the advocates of Qadar. Both Ma'bad and Ghaylān were executed by order of the caliph.

---

8. *Averroes on Plato's "Republic"*, pp. 8 f.

Free Will and Predestination

The controversy which pitted the advocates of free will and the predestinarians against each other has continued throughout Muslim history. According to Averroes, this controversy is "one of the most abstruse religious questions," because both the evidence of Scripture and that of reason appear to be contradictory. In the former case, because we find many statements in the Qu'ran which indicate that everything is determined or fore-ordained, and hence man is *compelled* (*mujbar*); while other statements indicate that man has a measure of free will or acquisition (*iktisāb*) in carrying out his decisions, and accordingly is not entirely compelled. He cites a series of Qu'ranic verses in support of both theses. Such verses as 54:49, which reads: "We created everything in measure (*qadar*)," and verse 57:22, which reads; "Not a disaster befalls on earth and in yourselves but is in a book," imply divine fore-ordination or compulsion. Set against these are other verses which speak of man's 'acquisition' of right or wrong actions for which he is liable to be rewarded or punished, such as verse 42:29, which reads: "That is due to what your hands have acquired," and verse 2:286, which reads: "It [the soul] gets rewarded for what it acquired and is called to account for the evil it acquired too."

Or take the Prophetic traditions, such as this *hadith* which reads: "Man is born in a state of nature; it is his parents who make him a Jew or a Christian." This tradition, according to Averroes, implies that man's disbelief (*kufr*) is the result of his upbringing; whereas his right belief (*imān*) is due to his original nature (*fiṭrah*). The *hadith*, however, is contradicted by this other saying of the Prophet in the words of the Almighty: "I have created these [people] for Paradise, hence they will perform the deeds of the people of Paradise, and I have created those others for Hell; hence they will perform the deeds of the people of Hell." This *hadith* clearly implies that disobedience or sin and unbelief are pre-determined by God.[9] It is for this reason, Averroes continues, that some Muslims, such as the Mu'tazilites, have maintained that man's acquisition is the cause of his pious or sinful actions, whereby he becomes liable to

9. *Al-Kashf,* p. 224.

reward or punishment; whereas others, such as the Determinists (*Jabriyah*) have maintained that man is thoroughly determined in his actions, or is compelled. The Ash'arites, he comments, have proposed an intermediate but meaningless position, according to which man has the power of 'acquisition;' but both the means of acquisition and the acquisition itself are created by God. "For if the acquisition itself and the acquired act," he writes, "are both created by God, then the individual [servant] is undoubtedly compelled in his acquisition."[10]

Added to the evidence of Scripture is the evidence of reason, or conflicting arguments which can be adduced in support of the one position or the other. Thus if man is said to be the doer or creator of his deeds, as the later Mu'tazilites actually put it, then certain actions or occurrences will happen contrary to God's will. This, says Averroes, would contradict the consensus of Muslims that there is no creator other than God.[11]

If, on the other hand, man is said to be fully compelled or determined in all his actions, then religious obligation (*taklīf*) would become a form of demanding the intolerable. Then there will be no difference between man and inanimate objects devoid of capacity (*istiṭā'ah*) altogether. It is for this reason, argues Averroes, that the majority of Muslims believe that capacity, as well as the power of sound reasoning, is a prerequisite of religious obligation. It was for this reason also that a leading Ash'arite, al-Juwayni, felt compelled to concede in his *Niẓāmiyah Epistle* that man has a certain measure of capacity, which he inferred from the impossibility of God demanding the intolerable. However, the early Ash'arites, Averroes rightly observes, allowed for the possibility of God demanding the intolerable, which the Mu'tazilites rejected as rationally abhorrent when predicated of the wise and just Creator.

To reconcile those two conflicting views, we should first understand, according to Averroes, that the aim of the religious lawgiver (*shāri'*) is not to oppose the one view to the other, but rather to mediate between them. For it appears that God Almighty has endowed us with certain faculties or powers, whereby we are able to perform actions of contrary natures.

10. *Ibid.*, pp. 224 f.
11. *Ibid.*, p. 225.

However, since 'acquiring' those actions (by which Averroes means performing them) is not possible unless outside causes or agents are propitious or cooperative, God has created such causes or agents in order to subserve us; whereupon the actions imputed to us will depend on the two factors or lines of determination, i.e. our own faculties and the external causes or agents. If this is the case, he writes, "then actions imputed to us also are done through our will and the propitiousness of the actions [or factors] from outside, and this is what is called God's decree (*qaḍā'*)."[12]

Averroes thus lays down two lines of determination, the human will or choice, and the concatenation of external causes or factors, determined ultimately by God's decree. For him, those two lines of determination are concurrent, rather than contradictory. What ensures the harmonious working of both our will and the external forces causing us to act is the perfect regularity of the order of causes and effects determined by God since all eternity. This order is not limited, Averroes observes, to the causes or factors lying outside us, but includes those causes which God has implanted in our bodies. Thus, "this determinate order of causes, both internal and external," he writes, "I mean this inerrancy, is the determination and decree (*qaḍā' wa qadar*) which God has prescribed for His servants and is synonymous with the Preserved Tablet."[13] Moreover, since the knowledge of the above-mentioned causes and the effects ensuing upon them necessarily is the exclusive prerogative of God, it follows that that knowledge is the cause of their very existence. That knowledge differs from our own in so far as it is the *cause* of the existence of everything known, while our knowledge is the *effect*, as he has argued in response to al-Ghazālī's charge that the philosophers deny God's knowledge of particulars.

The Ash'arites, with al-Ghazālī at their head, as we have seen, had objected to this answer on the ground that it presupposes that there are indeed secondary causes determining their effects necessarily, which they denied. In addition, that proposition runs counter to the consensus of Muslims that there is no other agent in the world except God, as

---

12. *Ibid.*, p. 226.
13. *Ibid.*, p. 227. The Preserved Tablet is the codex on which the Qu'ran has been written since all eternity. Cf. Qu'ran, 85:22.

al-Ghazālī had actually expressed it in the *Incoherence of the Philosophers* (Question 17); Averroes even refers to al-Ghazālī's argument in the *Revival of the Religious Sciences* (*al-Ihyā*) that one who applies to any animate or inanimate entity other than God the attribute of agent is like one who applies to the pen the attribute writer or writing, which is applicable exclusively to the human writer.

This analogy, according to Averroes, is not admissible. It would be admissible only if the writer were the inventor of the pen or its preserver in being, which is only true of God. For He alone is able to bring secondary causes into being and preserve them, together with their effects, for as long as He pleases. Thus the order we observe in nature is due to two factors:

1. The natures and properties of things which God has implanted in animate and inanimate entities.
2. The causes affecting those entities from outside, the most obvious being the motions of the heavenly bodies, which are subservient to us humans. "For, it is due to the order and regularity which the Creator imparted to their motions that our being and that of other things here below is preserved; so that were one to imagine the cessation of any of them, or to imagine it to be in another place or of another magnitude or speed than that which God has assigned to it, all the entities existing on the surface of the earth would cease to exist."[14]

Similarly, but for those faculties of nutrition and perception that God has placed in our bodies, as Galen and other philosophers and physicians attest, our own bodies would perish at once. This is borne out by such Qu'ranic verses as 16:12, which reads: "He has made the night and the day, the sun and the moon subservient to you," or verse 28:27, which reads: "It was out of His mercy that He created the night and the day for you, so that you may rest therein and seek some of His mercy."

We should also consider, he adds, how existing entities consist either of substances or of accidents. The former can only be created or invented by God Almighty, while the secondary causes associated with them can

14. *Al-Kashf*, p. 230.

simply affect the accidents which inhere in those substances. Thus semen or the menstrual fluid imparts to the woman the accident of heat; whereas the creation of the embryo and the spirit or life is the work of God alone. Similarly, the farmer cultivates the land and sows the seed, but the giver of form to the ear of wheat is God. It follows that in this sense there is no creator but God; since the actual entities created by God are the substances, not the accidents.

Moreover, the Ash'arite repudiation of the efficacy of causes by God's leave entails the repudiation of philosophy and science altogether. For science consists in the knowledge of things through the knowledge of their causes; while philosophy consists in the knowledge of their final causes. Such repudiation, he adds, is alien to human nature and entails the further incongruency that whoever repudiates the reality of causes in the visible world has no means of proving the existence of the Invisible Agent. "Thus those people (who deny causality) will have no means of knowing God Almighty, since they will not acknowledge that every action has an agent."[15] By the consensus of Muslims that there is no agent other than God, adduced by al-Ghazālī in support of his denial of causality, we should understand, according to Averroes, not that there are no agents whatsoever in the visible world, but rather that it is through the knowledge of those visible agents that we are led to discover the Invisible Agent. Once the existence of this Agent has been established, we become convinced that no other agent acts, except by His leave and good pleasure.

In conclusion, Averroes rejects both the libertarian position of the Mu'tazilites and the deterministic position of their rivals. The alleged 'intermediate' position of the Ash'arites is, for him, entirely meaningless, since the only sense they attach to man's 'acquisition' is the difference a man perceives between the voluntary motion of his hand and the involuntary motion of convulsion. But in so far as neither motion depends on us, we are not able to refrain from it, and therefore we are determined or compelled in both cases. Thus, the motion of convulsion and the allegedly voluntary, or 'acquired,' motion of the hand are identical in fact, the only difference between the two being purely semantic or verbal.

15. *Ibid.*, p. 232.

Relation of Ethics to Politics

If we return to the relation of ethics and politics, we will find, as already mentioned, that they are two parts of the same 'practical science.' In so far as man cannot achieve the two goals of practical and theoretical virtue without the assistance of his fellow men, the state arose in order to provide the conditions necessary for the pursuit of the good life. These conditions include provision for man's essential material needs, together with governance, which is a prerogative of the old, who have acquired in addition to the knowledge of the theoretical sciences, practical experience and prudence in the conduct of public affairs.

To inculcate virtue in the souls of the citizens by the rulers of the state, two methods are proposed, persuasion and coercion. Persuasion is described by Averroes as recourse to rhetorical and poetical arguments of the type used by Plato in the *Republic* in instructing the masses; whereas demonstration is reserved for the instruction of the select few. In the *Decisive Treatise (Faṣl al-Maqāl)*, Averroes is more explicit in distinguishing three methods of persuasion, the demonstrative suited for the philosophers or 'people of demonstration,' as he calls them, the dialectical method suited for the theologians or Mutakallimun, and the rhetorical suited for the masses at large. It is noteworthy that in the *Paraphrase of the Republic*, the poetical method replaces the dialectical.

Persuasion, Averroes goes on to explain, is natural and is suited chiefly for citizens who have grown up from their youth in the state under the tutelage of their wise elders. However, in dealing with enemies or those who are not amenable to the third type of rhetorical persuasion, recourse to coercion is justified, especially in dealing with non-virtuous citizens. As a last resort, recourse to war is justified, too. Such recourse, Averroes states, has been sanctioned by "this our divine law" (i.e. Islam), which stipulates that the ways "which lead to God, may He be exalted, are two: one of them is through speech and the other through war."[16] However, he does not give his sources in this context, but must be relying on the Qu'ranic stipulation itself that the infidels shall be summoned to accept Islam or else be prepared to fight to the death (Qu'ran 47:4).

16. *Averroes on Plato's "Republic"*, p. 12.

It is for this reason that Plato and Aristotle, Averroes continues, regard the two virtues of courage and wisdom as essential for the governance of the state, or its defense against foreign aggression. Here he refers to Plato's claim that of the two virtues, the Greeks excel in wisdom, which he does not contest, but judiciously comments: "Even if we accept that they [i.e. the Greeks] are the most disposed by nature to receive wisdom, we cannot disregard the fact that individuals like these, i.e. those disposed to wisdom, are frequently to be found [elsewhere]."[17] He then cites examples of countries, other than Greece, in which such individuals can be found, Syria, Iraq, Egypt and "this land of ours; namely Andalus," although less frequently than Greece.

The most effective way of instilling the virtues in the souls of the youth, he continues, is by combining bodily strength and keenness of sense, which are characteristic of the dog, to whom Plato compares the guardians. The dog is also characterized by the love of friends and the hatred of enemies. The first of these characteristics being unquestionably a philosophic one, Averroes infers from it the general maxim "that the guardians and the fighters ought to be by nature philosophers, lovers of knowledge, haters of ignorance, spirited, quick of movement, strong in body and with keen senses."[18] All of these are in fact canine qualities.

In practice, like Plato, Averroes recommends two arts, gymnastics and music, to ensure that the above virtues are instilled in the souls of the guardians. Gymnastics, he explains, is concerned with the inculcation of the bodily virtues, while music is concerned with inculcating psychic or intellectual virtues. By music, he explains, I mean "imitative arguments, having a melody from which the citizen receives discipline." For this reason, those arguments are subservient to poetry, which is particularly suited for the youth, who, when they have made enough progress, could be instructed or disciplined by recourse to the higher arguments, i.e. the rhetorical, the dialectical and finally the demonstrative.

However, recourse to imitation or the use of poetical similes should be carefully watched. In general, the guardians should use those imitations which are closest to the virtuous actions they intend to represent. Thus

17. *Ibid.*, p. 13.
18. *Ibid.*, p. 17. Cf. *Republic* II, 375A.

divine actions may be compared to political actions; natural or physical forms to voluntary actions or practical arts; intelligibles to sensibles and so on. He refers to Plato's argument that the worst imitations used in the teaching of children are untrue stories or fables, which can cause their souls the greatest harm. He cites as instances of those fables the mythological accounts of the Gods and the way in which they were supposed to take on human forms and deal treacherously with human beings.[19]

Other 'base imitations' mentioned by Averroes include the general maxim, entertained by the Mutakallimun of his day (by whom he unquestionably meant the Ash'arites), according to whom actions have no fixed character by themselves, but are good or bad by virtue of God's absolute fiat, as we have seen earlier in this chapter. From this, as Plato has stated explicitly, it would absurdly follow that God is the cause of both good and evil, which for Averroes entails a serious derogation from His perfection.[20]

Other false and harmful imitations mentioned by Averroes include stories or legends which speak of demons or angels, who are capable of assuming various forms, are invisible and can perform miraculous deeds. More abstract in character are such false imitations or representations of pleasure as the reward of virtue in the hereafter, and misery as punishment for vice. "For the virtues that come to pass from such imitations [or representations]," he writes, "are closer to being vices than virtues. Hence the moderate among them [i.e. the citizens of the state] is only moderate regarding pleasure, so as to obtain an even greater pleasure."[21] The same is true of the just who will not refrain from preying on the property of others out of a sense of duty, but rather in the expectation of greater rewards. Worse still, he will partake of acts of justice for the sake of base things, such as sensual or carnal pleasure. In such cases, "a man will be courageous, just, faithful and have virtues predicated of him, in order that he might copulate, drink and eat"[22] Averroes writes in obvious reference to the pleasures vouchsafed in the

19. Cf. *Republic* II, 380D.
20. *Averroes on Plato's "Republic"*, p. 20
21. *Ibid.*, p. 21.
22. *Ibid.*, p. 22.

Qu'ran to the faithful in the life-to-come. He refers in this connection to Plato's statement that the guardians, if they wish to be courageous, should not be frightened by forewarnings of the fate that awaits them after death. For then they would be more prone to accept a life of slavery, rather than die in war. Moreover, once the death of their comrades in the battlefield comes to pass, they should not lament them with 'women's songs' or weeping, which is worthy of weak souls only. Excessive laughter, he observes, should be condemned, like weeping, as a sign of weakness.

Unaware, perhaps, of Plato's devastating attack on the poets in the *Republic*, or indifferent to it, Averroes pursues the discussion of imitation in poetry, more in the spirit of Aristotelianism than Platonism. He interprets Plato to mean that the poets should avoid imitating base and vicious actions, and should dwell on noble and honorable actions instead. He then comments that Arabian poetry, by which he definitely meant pre-Islamic poetry, was of the descriptive type which dwelt on the imitation of the prancing of horses, the braying of asses, the roaring of thunder and the like, which ought to be banned from the ideal city. The general maxim he lays down in this connection is that only that type of poetry which serves a noble, moral purpose should be allowed, and the same goes for musical melodies or songs.

The care of the body, or gymnastics, should be governed by the same principle, according to Averroes. The guardians should be encouraged to partake of gymnastic exercises and simple foods which contribute to health and the disposition for war, and to avoid drinking. To ensure moderation in the consumption of food and the care of the body, it may be necessary to resort to physicians and judges, but "nothing is more indicative of the citizens' evil dispositions and baseness of their thoughts than their being in need of judges and physicians."[23] Medicine is allowed in the perfect city only in dire cases of casual injury, but not in the case of chronic defects. It is also allowed in the prescription of the kinds of foods suitable for the health of the body. Judges, on the other hand, are allowed only for the purpose of discriminating between bad and deficient natures among the young and those which can be disciplined or reformed. In the

23. *Ibid.*, p. 31.

former case, the judge will resort to execution, in the latter to castigation and counseling.

In choosing the head of the state from among the class of guardians, Averroes refers to Plato's fable, or 'noble lie,' according to which the members of that class should be told that they have all issued from the womb of mother earth, but with the nature of some of them gold was mixed, with that of others silver and with still others copper or iron; hence the different degrees of fitness to rule.[24] Naturally, the head of the state should be selected from the first or golden class, but it is not excluded that members of the class of silver could give birth to golden offspring who are fit to rule.

Characteristics of the Ruler or Philosopher–King

The head of the state should, therefore, be chosen from the first or golden class and should be most virtuous, most disciplined, steadfast and undeterred in his dedication to the noblest cause of ruling the state. In addition, he should not be allowed to own private property and covet gold or other forms of wealth, which is the root of all animosity and strife within the state. To guard against coveting gold, the ruler will be told that he has no need of it, since it is already mixed with his own original nature. This admonition will apply to a lesser extent to the two lower classes of artisans and laborers, whose natures are mixed with silver and copper. Like Plato, Averroes accords to women an equal share in the management of the affairs of the state. "And we say," he writes, "that women, in so far as they are of one kind with men, necessarily share in the end of man. They will differ only in less or more," that is, in degree.[25] Hence they should be allowed to engage in warfare with men, as was the case with bedouin women (in pre-Islamic times). It is even possible for women to rise to the rank of philosophers and rulers, according to Averroes.

Sexual relations or copulation between men and women should be governed by the principles Plato had laid down; the union of the sexes should only be allowed during certain seasons and among couples best

24. Cf. *Republic* III, 414.
25. *Averroes on Plato's "Republic"*, p. 57.

suited to produce the finest offspring. The community of women, according to Averroes, requires that men and women should dwell together, but without copulation out of season.[26] It is significant that on some of these points, especially the rights of women to share in male activities, particularly warfare, Averroes is clearly in agreement with Plato. On the more delicate issues, such as the community of women and property, he resorts to the purely narrative style, simply reporting what Plato has said in the *Republic.*

The characteristics of the ruler or philosopher–king identified by Averroes, along essentially al-Fārābian lines, with the lawgiver (i.e. the prophet), the Imam, or caliph are then given as follows:

1. Love of knowledge and the aptitude to acquire the theoretical sciences and to teach them.
2. Good retention, as a prerequisite of learning.
3. Love of learning and yearning for it at all times.
4. Love of truth and hatred of falsehood.
5. Contempt for sensual pleasures.
6. Aversion to amassing wealth and the desire for it.
7. Magnanimity, or the yearning for the knowledge of all things.
8. Courage.
9. Resolve to pursue on his own whatever is good or beautiful.
10. Eloquence or the facility of expressing his thoughts.
11. The ability to light quickly on the middle term.[27]

With respect to the goal of man in this world, some regard it, Averroes observes, as self-preservation, others as pleasure, still others as honor or speculative pursuits. The "law existing in our time," by which he obviously meant the Islamic law or *sharīʿah*, stipulates that the goal of man is complete compliance with what God wills, and the only way through which that is known is prophethood. What God wills, he then explains, is for us to seek to know Him and pursue virtuous actions, as philosophy also teaches. Here he criticizes the (Ashʿarite) Mutakallimun for denying that actions have any intrinsic properties of right or wrong, and for

26. *Ibid.,* p. 61.
27. *Ibid.,* pp. 71–74. Cf. *Republic* VI, 485.

reducing those two moral categories exclusively to the divine decree, as we have seen.

When he proceeds to define the goal of man in more specific terms, Averroes tends to incline to the Aristotelian view that this end is happiness (*eudaimonia*), which he defines as an "activity of the rational soul in accordance with what is required by virtue.[28] But since the parts of the rational soul are two, theoretical and practical, man's perfection is twofold also. However, practical activity is subservient to the theoretical, and accordingly moral perfection is ultimately a means to man's ultimate perfection, which is theoretical or intellectual. That perfection is achieved in the last analysis when the human intellect, after passing through the preliminary stages of habitual and acquired thought, is 'conjoined' to the Active Intellect. Significantly, Averroes, who was critical of the Neoplatonists, especially Avicenna, was willing to grant that conjunction with the Active Intellect of Neoplatonic cosmology that exalted role as the consummation of the human process of intellection.[29]

Degeneration of the Perfect State

After outlining, in the manner of Plato, the way in which the ideal state, or as it had been called since the time of al-Fārābī, the 'virtuous city,' should be built, he proceeds in the concluding parts of his *Paraphrase* to discuss the way in which such a perfect state is liable to degenerate into its opposite. It degenerates first, as Plato also held, into timocracy, in which the primary goal of the ruler is no longer virtue or wisdom, but rather honor; then into plutocracy or oligarchy in which the primary goal is the acquisition of wealth. The oligarchic state degenerates next into democracy and finally into tyranny. Like Plato, Averroes recognizes that the timocratic state is the nearest to the perfect or aristocratic state; but the timocratic ruler, he observes, has a tendency to lord it over his fellow-citizens or subjects. In plutocracy or oligarchy, the wealthiest section of the population, who are generally the few, tend to rule. In democracy, contrariwise, it is the majority who tend to rule in an unrestrained

28. *Ibid.*, p. 84.
29. *Ibid.*, pp. 93 f.

manner. "Hence all the arts and dispositions emerge in this city (state), and it is so disposed that from it may emerge the virtuous city and every one of the other cities,"[30] as Plato actually held. Despite his intense dislike for democracy, the latter conceded in the *Republic* that democracy had this merit that it resembled "a garment of many colours . . . and a bazaar [or emporium] of constitutions, from which city-builders can choose freely."[31] For Averroes, democracy was the first to grow out of the 'city of necessity,' as al-Fārābī had called this primordial state, in which people were primarily concerned with providing for the necessities of life. In time, the democratic state evolved into the 'city of the mighty,' as Averroes calls it, and as was the case with the ancient Persian state and "many of the cities of ours," i.e. in al-Andalus, as he says. Then the multitude is plundered by the mighty and the democratic state eventually degenerates into tyranny or despotism.[32]

The characteristic feature of the tyrannical state is that the aim of the ruler in it is self-aggrandizement by means of seeking honor, wealth, pleasure or a combination of all three, and in the process reducing his fellow-citizens or subjects to the status of slaves, pandering to his wishes or desires. As an example of the degeneration of the virtuous or perfect state into the timocratic, Averroes cites the earliest Muslim caliphate, known as that of the Orthodox or Upright caliphs (*al-Rāshidūn*) (632–661), which was succeeded by the Umayyad state, founded by Mu'āwiyah in 661. He compares that state to "the governance existing in these lands [of al-Andalus]."[33]

Sometimes, Averroes adds, the timocratic state degenerates into the hedonistic, whose rulers are primarily motivated to seek pleasure. He cites as an example of the hedonistic state that of Almoravids, founded by the Berber chief Yūsuf Ibn Tafshīn (d. 1107). At first, members of that dynasty imitated the 'city of the law,' but after the death of its founder, it was transformed into a timocratic state under his son. It was later transformed into the hedonistic state and finally

30. *Ibid.*, p. 110.
31. *Republic* VIII, 557D.
32. *Averroes on Plato's "Republic"*, p. 112.
33. *Ibid.*, p. 121.

perished. It was succeeded by the Almohades dynasty, under whose rule Averroes lived and which he describes as one based on "the governance of the law."[34]

Interestingly, Averroes applies those genetic principles in some detail to the political situation in al-Andalus during his lifetime and shortly before. Democracy degenerated into tyranny during the reign of the grandson of the founder of Almoravids dynasty, 'Ali Ibn Yūsuf, between 1106 and 1145 in Cordova. That dynasty was overthrown in 1146 by 'Abd al-Mu'min, founder of the successor Berber dynasty Almohades.

Be this as it may, in his detailed account of the degeneration of democracy into tyranny, Averroes explains, along essentially Platonic lines, that it is due to their desire for absolute freedom, and the lawlessness ensuing upon it, that the masses in democracy are progressively weakened, whereupon they are subdued by the class of 'drones' or opportunists, who thrive on the exploitation of the moneyed class, as real drones thrive on honey. Thus subdued, the masses seek their salvation at the hands of the strongest man among them. Before long this would-be savior proceeds to concentrate power in his own hands and that of his coterie, plunder the subjects who elected him in the first place, and tyrannize them. At that point, the masses turn against this tyrant, who in order to secure his hold on the state turns to "wicked foreigners," from whom he recruits his bodyguard.

The Tunisian philosopher of history, Ibn Khaldūn (d. 1406), who was conversant with Averroes' work, especially his juridical writings as a fellow-Maliki scholar, has given a similar account of the way in which the perfect rule of the Orthodox caliphs was transformed into a timocracy at the hands of the Umayyads and how the Abbasid caliphate eventually succumbed to the foreign mercenaries that the Abbasid caliph, al-Mu'tasim (d. 842) had recruited in his bodyguard for the first time.[35]

---

34. *Ibid.*, p. 125.
35. *Al-Muqaddimah*, p. 205.

9

Averroes as Jurist and Physician

Juridical and Rational Deduction (Qiyās)

Averroes may be said to have outstripped all his predecessors among the philosophers of the East, in two major respects. In the first instance, none of them had contributed significantly to the theological–philosophical controversy which was at the center of the intellectual and religious life of Muslims from the time they came into contact with Greek philosophy and 'the foreign sciences' in the middle of the eighth century. As we have already seen, the contribution of Averroes to this controversy was outstanding and decisive. In the second instance, none of them had contributed to the more religiously pertinent subject of jurisprudence (*fiqh*), which together with Qur'anic exegesis (*tafsīr*) and Prophetic Tradition (Ḥadith), was regarded as an essential part of the task of giving a coherent account of the Islamic system of beliefs, with its theoretical and practical components.

Averroes is known from the bibliographical sources to have written a number of treatises on jurisprudence, including the *Primer of the Discretionary Scholar* (*Bidāyat al-Mujtahid*), a summary of al-Ghazālī's *al-Mustasfa* (*Gist of Jurisprudence*), a short tract on *Sacrifices* and another on *Land tax*. Of these treatises, the *Primer* is particularly valuable in introducing the reader to his concept of the nature and aims of the science of jurisprudence.

In the opening chapter, Averroes explains that his aim in writing this treatise is "to give an inventory of the juridical decisions on which scholars are in agreement and those on they are in disagreement, by recourse to those principles and rules which are regarded as fundamental."[1] He observes next that such an inventory should be preceded by a discussion of the diverse methods used in making legal decisions, their various kinds, and the causes of dissent among scholars. He reduces those methods to the three received from the Prophet; namely, utterance, exercise and tacit concurrence. The first refers to what the Prophet enunciated in specific terms; the second to his practical solution of legal disputes and the third to what was the subject of tacit approval (*taqrīr*) on his part. This leads Averroes to engage in the discussion of those decisions on which the Prophet as lawgiver was silent. With respect to these decisions, the majority of scholars, he notes, have held that they should be settled by recourse to analogy (*qiyās*).

The method of analogy, it will be recalled, was at the center of the controversy between those scholars, who like Mālik Ibn Anas (d. 795) and Ahmad Ibn Ḥanbal (d. 855), founders of the Malikite and Ḥanbalite legal schools (sing. *madhhab*), respectively, tended to restrict its scope; and those who like the founders of the rival Ḥanafi and Shāfiʿi schools tended to extend this scope. The first group are generally referred to as the people of Tradition (*Hadith*), the latter as the 'people of opinion' (*raʾy*). Some like the literalist (*zāhiri*) Ibn Ḥazm (d. 1086) went so far as to reject the use of analogy (*qiyās*) in any form or guise. In their view what the Prophet did not legislate for is not a legitimate object of legal decision; the only legitimate basis for such decisions being textual, i.e. the Qurʾan or the Hadith.

Averroes next discusses the legal utterances, which he divides into four categories, three of which are objects of consensus (*ijmāʿ*) and the fourth an object of dissent. The first of the three types which are objects of consensus consists of utterances or statements which are generally understood; the second consists of statements which are particularly understood; the third of general statements bearing on a particular case or particular statement, indicating a general principle. An instance of the first category is the

1. *Bidāyat* I, p. 325.

prohibition in the Qur'an (5:3) of the eating of pig, which, scholars are unanimous, refers to all kinds of pig. An example of the second category is the Qur'anic injunction to "take alms of their property voluntarily" (Qur'an 9:103), which does not apply to all forms of property; while an example of the third category, or particular statements indicating general principles, is the Qur'anic verse 17:23, which orders children "not to say fie to their parents," since this order excludes all forms of parental abuse.

By contrast, the fourth type of legal utterances or statements consists in understanding the connotation of a positive statement as excluding its negative, or inferring from negating a decision the affirmation of its opposite. This, Averroes observes, is a principle which is open to question. An example thereof is the Prophet's statement that "alms-giving is required with respect to sheep on the loose." Some have interpreted this statement to mean that alms are stipulated only in the case of sheep on the loose, which is clearly questionable. For Averroes, this statement should not be understood in a restrictive sense.

Qiyās, which was used by the logicians to mean deduction and by the jurists to mean analogy is next discussed. He begins by defining legal *qiyās* here as "applying a decision regarding a given subject juridically to another subject on which Scripture is silent, either because of its analogy to what Scripture has enunciated . . . or on account of a cause which is common to them both."[2] We have thus two forms of legal deduction, analogical and causal.

In the *Decisive Treatise* (*Faṣl al-Maqāl*), as we have seen in an earlier chapter, Averroes draws a parallel between legal and rational *qiyās* and defends the use of the latter on the ground that, just as the jurist is justified in using it in legal decisions, the seeker of truth (*'ārif*) may resort to its counter part or rational deduction in settling theological or philosophical disputes. Thus, he may deduce from the (Qur'anic) injunction to investigate existing entities the obligation to know the meaning of rational deduction and its varieties.[3] That is how Averroes had in fact defined philosophy earlier in that treatise as: "the investigation of existing entities and their consideration in so far as they manifest the Maker; I

2. *Ibid.*, p. 328.
3. *Faṣl al-Maqāl*, p. 30.

mean, in so far as they are made. For existing entities manifest the Maker, in so far as they are known to be made."[4]

The verbal methods, which involve an explicit textual utterance, as mentioned above, consist either in a command, a prohibition or a choice. If the command is understood to be definitive and penalty attaches to ignoring it, then it is obligatory. If, on the other hand, it is understood to entail reward for obeying it and penalty is precluded, then it is an exhortation (*nadb*). The prohibition, contrariwise, could also be understood as definitive in such a way that ignoring it would entail a penalty, and then it is called a ban. If it is understood to mean warning the agent off the action, without reference to penalty, then it is called an admonition. Hence, the types of religious or legal decisions which can be derived from the five methods already mentioned are: obligatory, exhortatory, banned, admonished and voluntary. The last is synonymous with the permissible.[5]

Averroes lists, next, the six causes of the basic incongruencies resulting from the improper use of the five methods. The first consists in mistaking the general for the particular term, the particular for the general or misunderstanding them. The second consists in equivocation, as when a command is understood to refer to obligation or exhortation, and prohibition is understood to refer to what is banned or simply to what is repugnant. The third consists in grammatical error; the fourth in mistaking the figurative for the real use of the term. The fifth consists in using the term in an absolute sense at times and in a relative sense at other times; the sixth in the "opposition in the two cases to all the types of terms upon which decisions are based jointly," whether in point of action or concurrence. The same holds in the case of the deductions or analogies themselves, or that of the opposition which results from all the utterances pertaining to the action, the concurrence or deduction. The same holds in the case of the opposition of the action to the concurrence, deduction or vice versa.[6]

From these methodological explanations, it is clear that Averroes as a jurist was anxious to stress the role of analogy or deduction in settling legal

---

4. *Ibid.*, p. 27.
5. *Bidāyat* I, p. 331.
6. *Ibid.*, p. 332.

disputes, rather than be content with recourse to the authority of accredited scholars or judges, as traditionalists tended to do. Thus, in the *Decisive Treatise*, he draws a parallel between juridical and rational deduction, rejecting the view that, since the latter was introduced in the wake of the first generation of Muslims, it should be dismissed as an innovation. For so was the former. Moreover, he writes, "most of our coreligionists are in agreement, except for a small group of literalists, whose position is discredited by the texts [of the Qur'an]."[7] For the Qur'an has repeatedly called upon mankind to investigate the nature of reality, as a means of knowing God as Creator of the world, as mentioned earlier.

It follows, he goes on, that Scripture itself has urged us to resort to rational and juridical deductions with their many varieties. If it should turn out that the study of rational deduction has not been attempted by our Muslim predecessors but has been thoroughly investigated by the ancients (i.e. Greeks), then it is incumbent on us to shoulder this responsibility, especially in the case of rational deduction, which has been thoroughly investigated by our predecessors, by whom Averroes obviously meant the ancient philosophers or logicians.

If it is objected, he hastens to add, that that investigation has been attempted by people of a different religious affiliation, prior to the rise of Islam, we would answer that the type of instrument (*ālah*) used in slaughtering the beast is irrelevant to the validity of the sacrifice. The same is true of the kind of method, whether foreign or not, used in deduction. For, if we find that "all that is needed with respect to rational deductions has been investigated by the ancients in the most perfect manner," it becomes incumbent on us to accept it. If, contrariwise, it is found to contain what is not right, we ought to draw attention to it. In broader terms, it is our duty, when we find in the writings of the ancients that which conforms to the rules of logical demonstration, "to accept it and thank them for it. If it does not accord with truth, we should draw attention to it, warn against it and excuse its [authors]."[8]

It is not only in the fields of logic or speculative thought that we are dependent on the discoveries of our predecessors, Averroes explains,

7. *Fasl al-Maqāl*, pp. 30 f.
8. *Ibid.*, p. 32.

but in all other fields of enquiry, including mathematics and astronomy. For without such discoveries, we would be completely at a loss in answering the simplest questions. The same is true of the science of jurisprudence, since it was perfected after a long period of time; so that were one to begin to learn by himself all the arguments developed by legal scholars throughout the Muslim world, he would become a laughing stock.[9]

Legal Problems and Decisions

The substantive discussion of legal problems begins with the question of ritual cleanliness (*tahārb*), which, Averroes notes, is the customary procedure of eminent jurists. Like those jurists, he distinguishes two types of cleanliness, one from defecation and the other from contact with something unclean. The chief means of cleanliness in the first case is ritual washing (*wuḍū*), as the Qur'an, Hadith and *ijmāʿ* stipulate.[10] With respect to the second case, he mentions the different Prophetic traditions and opinions of scholars, such as Mālik, al-Shāfiʿi and others, without expressing a personal opinion. A classic case of ritual uncleanliness is then discussed, namely, the touching of women. Here Averroes reviews the views of various scholars, some of whom, he states, held that whoever touches a woman or kisses her should wash, while others laid down as a condition of uncleanliness that kissing should be attended by a sensation of pleasure. To account for such differences among scholars, he refers to the ambiguity of the two terms for touch in the Arabic language, i.e. *lams* and *mass*, which can mean touching by hand or copulation. The chief argument of the first group, he states, is that where a term admits of two connotations, the real and figurative, the real or obvious meaning should be preferred. The advocates of the second opinion, however, hold that both connotations of the term 'touch' should be understood. Averroes' own opinion appears to be that it is uncommon in Arabic usage for the real and figurative meanings of a term to be taken in conjunction, which he says, is self-evident. In other words, he appears to favor the view of the

9. *Ibid.*, p. 33.
10. *Bidāyat* I, p. 335.

first group of scholars, who limited touching in the Qur'an and the Traditions to touching by hand.[11]

The remaining parts of the *Primer* deal with miscellaneous legal questions of the conventional type, such as contracts, prayer, fasting, marriage, divorce, crime, punishment, adultery, food and drink, alms-giving and pilgrimage. Averroes' method, as distinct from the termino-logical and methodological discussion given in the preparatory parts of the book, consists in reporting the pertinent Prophetic traditions and the testimony of the Companions of the Prophet (*Sahābah*), including 'Ali Ibn Abī Tālib, the Shi'ite Imam. This is followed by the divergent opinions of the founders of the four legal schools of jurisprudence (*madhāhib*), Mālik Ibn Anas, Ahmad Ibn Hanbal, al-Shāfi'i and Abū Hanīfah.

In his discussion of holy war (*jihād*), for instance, he refers to the consensus of scholars that it is not a universal obligation, but is supererogatory where freemen are concerned, but not slaves. The enemies against whom holy war is prescribed, he explains, are said to be all polytheists (*mushrikūn*) by the generality of scholars, with the exception of Mālik, who excluded the Ethiopians and the Turks on the basis of a Prophetic tradition, although Mālik himself could not vouch for its authenticity.[12] He then refers to the rules governing the treatment of non-Muslims. All polytheists, old or young, male or female, he states, are liable to enslavement, with the exception of monks (*ruhbān*). Whether the wives and children of polytheists may be killed is dismissed on the basis of a Prophetic tradition, unless they have taken part in fighting Muslims. Similarly, hermits, blind men, lunatics and the old should be spared.

On the question of the poll-tax (*jiziyah*), Averroes reviews the opinions of the various scholars. Some of them, he mentions, held that it should be levied from all polytheists, others have limited it to the People of the Book, or Jews or Christians, as well as Manicheans (*Majūs*), also on the basis of a Prophetic tradition.[13]

11. *Ibid.*, p. 496.
12. *Ibid.*, III, p. 411.
13. *Ibid.*, p. 442.

Marriage, Divorce and Adultery

As one would expect, a large part of the book is devoted to the questions of marriage, divorce and adultery. In the fourth part, he begins by discussing the terms of the marital contract (*'aqd*) and explains that consent, an essential condition of this contract, is verbally expressed by non-virgin women, and by silent consent in the case of virgins. However, refusal should be verbally expressed in both cases. Whether the marital contract requires a sponsor (*wali*), we are told, has been an object of controversy, some requiring it, others not.

With respect to divorce, Averroes refers to two varieties, definitive, which must be uttered thrice, and revocable, in which the husband can demand the wife's return, provided she has not married another man in the interval. As for divorce by uttering the formula, "You are divorced," three times, Averroes refers to the different opinions of scholars regarding this mode of divorce. He cites the opinion of the majority of scholars, who have allowed it, provided the intent of the husband is clear and definite.[14] He mentions that the tripartite formula does not require an actual intention, according to Mālik and Abū Ḥanīfah. Sometimes, he mentions, the divorce can be effected by using covert, rather than overt or explicit utterances, which render the divorce implicitly final. For instance, instead of saying to the wife: "You are divorced (*anti tāliq*)" three times, the husband might say: "You are no longer my lawful wife," the implication being that the form of words is not important.

Whether marriage to an adulteress is lawful is then discussed. The Qur'an (24:3) states that an adulteress can only be married to an adulterer or polytheist (*mushrik*), but not a Muslim. The generality of scholars, Averroes explains, understood this verse to indicate disapproval (*dham*) rather than prohibition. He then quotes a Prophetic tradition according to which someone told the Prophet that his wife was promiscuous, to which the Prophet replied: "Divorce her." The man then said: "But I love her," to which the Prophet replied: "Then keep her."[15]

14. *Ibid.*, IV, p. 348.
15. *Ibid.*, p. 375.

On the question of the sanctions against adultery, Averroes begins by listing the four kinds of adulterer/adulteress, followed by the sanctions appropriate to each. The types of adulterer/adulteress are married men/ women, maidens (non-virgins) and virgins, freemen and slaves. The sanctions are then given as stoning, whipping and expulsion. Free maidens are generally believed to be deserving of stoning. As to whether they should be whipped prior to stoning, the scholars, we are told, are in disagreement. The majority have precluded whipping, but al-Ḥasan al-Basri, for one, allowed it.[16]

Averroes next discusses the various opinions of scholars and the Prophetic traditions cited in support of their conflicting views on the subject of sanctions against adultery. As for virgins, he states, the consensus of Muslims is that they should be whipped a hundred lashes, as stipulated in the Qur'an (verse 24:2). Some have added to whipping, as he mentions, expulsion for a whole year. The sanction in the case of slaves, male or female, according to verse 4:25, is half that meted out to freemen and free women.

Determining the guilt is either by way of confession on the part of the culprit or the testimony of four just witnesses, Averroes states. However, forced adultery or rape is not punishable, according to the majority of scholars.[17]

It is to be noted that in the discussion of sanctions and the categories of culprits, Averroes does not express any personal opinion, but is content to report the opinions of accredited scholars, as well as the evidence of the Qur'an and Prophetic traditions (Hadith).

In his discussion of polygamy, Averroes mentions that the consensus of Muslims is that marrying four women is lawful for a freeman, but not a slave, although both Mālik and Abū Ḥanifah, we are told, contested the latter provision. Mālik and the Literalists (*Ahl al-Ẓāhir*), he states, allowed that a slave could marry four women, Abū Ḥanifah allowed only two.[18]

These instances are enough, we believe, to illustrate Averroes' method of exposition as jurist. He is extremely thorough in citing Qur'anic

16. *Ibid.*, VI, p. 115.
17. *Ibid.*, p. 136.
18. *Ibid.*, p. 277.

passages, Prophetic traditions and opinions of accredited scholars, especially the founders of the four legal schools. When he expresses his own opinion, he does not always favor the Māliki view, despite the fact that he served as a Māliki judge at Seville and chief judge at Cordova, as we have seen. The obvious contrast between Averroes as a philosopher–theologian and as a jurist is that in the first case his approach tends to be thoroughly rational or discursive. Sometimes, in his commentaries, however, he is very textual, especially in the larger commentaries. In his juridical writings, his methodology is also often textual or narrative. He explicitly sought, as we have seen, to define the points of opposition or parallelism between the juridical and philosophical methods of *qiyās*. In this respect, he seems to follow in the footsteps of the founder of the Almohades dynasty, Ibn Tumart, who tried to defend the use of deduction in theology in the face of the Almoravids' opposition, as we have seen in an earlier chapter. Averroes is known to have written a commentary on the creed (*'aqīdah*) of Ibn Tumart, which illustrates this point.

Averroes' Medical Writings

Averroes, who served as physician royal at the court of Abū Ya'qūb Yūsuf, following the death of Ibn Ṭufayl, has left a large number of medical treatises, the best-known of which is *al-Kulliyāt fi'l-Ṭibb* (*General Principles of Medicine*), written around 1162, about seven years prior to his introduction in 1169 to the caliph, which launched him on his career as a commentator of Aristotle. His other medical treatises included his commentary on Avicenna's medical poem, known as *Sharh al-Urjūzah*, and a large number of summaries (*talākhīs*) of Galen's medical treatises, including *On the Humours*, *On Natural Powers*, *On Diseases and Symptoms*, *On Fever*, *On the Elements*, *On Medications* and *On Hygiene*. These treatises were published in 1987 in a critical edition by Fr. George S. Anawāti and Sa'īd Zāyid.

Al-Kulliyāt was translated into Latin as *Colliget*, and was used as a medical textbook in Europe for centuries. As its name implies, it deals with the general principles of medicine, as against particular matters, with which, we are told, his friend and colleague Marwān Ibn Zuhr had dealt in his *al-Taysīr* (*Simplification*) at Averroes' own request. Thus, he defines medicine in *al-Kulliyāt* as "an effective art, based on true principles and concerned with preserving man's health and abating disease, as far as possible, in dealing with individual bodies. Thus the aim of this art is not to heal necessarily, but rather to do what ought to be done, to the extent possible and within the time-span needed."[19] He then indicates the relation of medicine, in its theoretical aspects, with physics, in so far as they deal with causal principles common to them both, such as the elements, to the extent that they affect the health or sickness of the body. The practical part of medicine, which includes the arts of anatomy and experimental medicine, differs from the theoretical, in so far as experience and pharmacology, or *materia medica*, enter into it. However, he stresses the role of reasoning in medicine and argues, as Galen had done in a treatise which was known to the Arabs, that indeed a good physician is necessarily a philosopher. It follows that the art of medicine in general admits of three divisions corresponding to the knowledge of the subject-matter, the aims intended by such knowledge and finally, the means whereby such aims can be attained.

However, despite his insistence on the correlation of medicine and philosophy, including logic, Averroes believed that "the acquisition of the universal principles of this art, coupled with prolonged experience ... will enable [the physician] to acquire a series of empirical premises which are essential to the art of healing."[20]

In the pathological part of *al-Kulliyāt*, and in *Sharh al-Urjūzah*, the commentary on Avicenna's medical poem, Averroes defines disease as a condition "whereby it acts or is affected contrary to the natural order."[21] Symptoms, on the other hand, are defined as conditions which ensue upon disease and are, accordingly, the physician's pointers to disease, in so far as the latter is the cause of the symptom or symptoms in question. Some principal diseases and the symptoms corresponding to them are then given as follows:

1. Persistent headaches resulting in migraine, which could cause disorders of the eyes.

19. *Al-Kulliyāt*, p. 19.
20. *Ibid.*, p. 21.
21. *Ibid.*

2. Redness of face and eyes, accompanied by swelling, lacrimation and aversion to light, resulting in possible swelling in the brain.
3. Nightmares and vertigo which sometimes lead to epilepsy.
4. Repeated bouts of pneumonia which may lead to consumption.
5. Excessive obesity which may lead to bleeding or heart attack and instant death.
6. Dilution of the lower abdomen and the sides, which could lead to an affection of the kidneys.
7. Redness of the face and shortness of breath, accompanied by loss of voice, which could lead to leprosy.[22]

In addition to bodily or physical symptoms, Averroes refers in *al-Kulliyāt* to psychological symptoms attendant on affections of the brain and, as a result, interfering with the mental functions of imagination, reflection and memory. Those diseases are caused by a deficiency of either the choleric or melancholic humors. When the choleric humor dominates, hallucinations arise; whereas when the melancholic dominates, anxiety, fear and suspiciousness arise for no apparent reason. However, when the patient dreams of seas and waters, and complains of nightmares and bad digestion, these symptoms are consequent upon affections of the phlegmatic humor. Similarly, swelling of the brain and excessive passion (*'ishq*) may be due to a disorder of the humors.[23]

In the discussion of the factors conducive to preserving health, Averroes argues in his summary of Galen's book *On Hygiene* that there are really two chief ways: a good digestion and a sound bowel-movement. The first consists in choosing those foods which are appropriate in point of quality, quantity, time and frequency. Those include a balanced diet consisting of leavened bread, meat of mutton, birds and fish. Fruits should be avoided, except for ripe figs and grapes, and so should herbs. Exercise is recommended following proper digestion, and bathing following exercise, but before eating.

22. *Ibid.*, pp. 111 f.
23. *Ibid.*, p. 145.

Galen and Aristotle

Despite his obvious interest in Galen, as shown by the large number of summaries or paraphrases of his works listed above, Averroes tends to be critical of that Alexandrian physician's stand on a variety of questions, especially where philosophy and medicine intersect. Where Galen's views are in conflict with Aristotle's on physical or related questions, Averroes invariably defends Aristotle and criticizes Galen. As an instance of his Aristotelian bias, we might mention his comments on Galen's references to those philosophers and physicians who have argued that mankind derives from a single element or nature, basing themselves on the thesis that the four elements are capable of transformation into each other.[24] Thus, those who believed fire to be the first principle, like Heraclitus, held that mankind derives ultimately from fire; whereas those who believed that it is air, like Anaximines, referred man's genesis to water. Galen has charged Parmenides and Melissus, the Eleatic philosophers, with the same reductionism; since for them being is numerically one. Both Galen and Hippocrates rejected these monistic views of the origin of mankind. They agreed with Aristotle that the four primary elements enter into the composition of all natural entities, including man's body; in addition, they held, like Aristotle, that those elements are not reducible into each other. Here, as one would expect, Averroes is in agreement with both ancient physicians, in so far as they agreed with Aristotle.

To illustrate further Averroes' Aristotelian leanings, we may mention his discussion of the views of the philosophers, by whom he meant the Peripatetics, and those of the physicians, by whom he meant Galen, Hippocrates and others, regarding therapy, as given in his summary of Galen's treatise, the *Art of Healing*. The physicians, he explains, base their view of therapy on the maxim that the opposite heals its opposite and the like heals its like. The philosophers, contrariwise, base their view on the principle that healing, like any natural or artificial process, consists in the progress from one given principle to another, in accordance with a fixed procedure directed towards a desired result. Not only in therapy, but in all other medical procedures, argues Averroes, the same natural process or

24. Hīlat al-Bur', in *Rasā'il Ibn Rushd*, pp. 433 f.

transition from a determinate state to another, occurs, and although art imitates nature in this respect, the ways of nature are superior. Thus in the restoration of health, recourse to natural methods of healing, such as exercise, bathing, massage and the like, are more effective than artificial procedures, such as medication, surgery and the like. Averroes writes, in conclusion, that: "When the physician treats a patient in any way at all, he is really assisting nature according to a determinate course of action and towards a determinate goal. That goal is either of the same type as the disease or that of health. If the physician is ignorant of that course or that goal . . . and treats the patient in a haphazard way, he will be essentially at fault and is right only by accident."[25] Such a physician will tend to be successful in very rare cases and will fail in most cases. That is why Aristotle is quoted by Averroes as saying (in *Parva Naturalia*) that most patients who die actually die by reason of medicine, or rather the physician's fault.

Whatever Aristotle's intent in this quotation, Averroes agreed with him that philosophical learning, especially in logic and physics, is an essential prerequisite of mastering the theory and practice of medicine.

---

25. *Ibid.*, p. 438.

10

Averroes and the Latin West

The Efflorescence of Philosophical Studies in al-Andalus

It is fairly well-known, as was mentioned in the Introduction, that following the fall of the Roman Empire in 476, Europe entered a period of cultural decline, sometimes referred to as the Dark Ages. That period was marked by an almost total ignorance of the great cultural legacy of the Greeks in philosophy, medicine and science. During the Hellenistic and Roman periods that legacy had been perpetuated by a number of distinguished philosophers, scientists and physicians, such as Cicero (d. 43 B.C.E.), Euclid (fl. 300 B.C.E.), Archimedes (d. 212 B.C.E.), Galen (d. 200), Epicetus (d. 135), Marcus Aurelius (d. 180), Plotinus and Proclus. In the Byzantine Empire, the struggle between Christianity and Greek philosophy culminated in 529 in the closure of the School of Athens.

In the western parts of the Empire, Greek learning was almost completely forgotten by the sixth century; the only philosophical works accessible to Western scholars between the sixth and twelfth centuries were Aristotle's logical works, as translated by the Roman consul, Beothius, to which Porphyry's famous *Isagoge*, or *Introduction to Logic* was added. Of Plato's works, only parts of his great cosmological Dialogue, the *Timaeus*, had been translated by Chalcidus, in the fourth century, as was mentioned in the Introduction.

By contrast, in the Near East and Persia, the Greek and Hellenistic legacies in philosophy, science and medicine, coupled with the Indian and ancient Persian legacies in mathematics and literary lore, were being gradually assimilated by the Syriacs, Persians and Arabs, at the major centers of learning at Jundishapur in Persia, Edessa, Antioch and Nisibin in Syria, and elsewhere. However, this process of cultural assimilation of the so-called 'ancient sciences' received added momentum during the Abbasid caliphate (750–1285). Many of the leading members of that caliphate, such as al-Mansūr, Hārūn al-Rashīd, and especially his son al-Ma'mūn, took an active part in patronizing the work of scholars, who hailed from the four corners of the Abbasid empire. Thus during the eighth and ninth centuries almost all the medical works of Galen and Hippocrates, the *Geometry* of Euclid, the whole of the Aristotelian corpus with the exception of the *Politics*, and a number of Platonic dialogues in the 'synopses' of Galen were translated into Arabic. In addition a large number of commentaries on Aristotle's works by Nicolaus of Damascus, Alexander of Aphrodisias, Themistius and Olympiodorus, a paraphrase of the *Enneads* of Plotinus, and the *Elements of Theology* by Proclus were accessible to Arabic-speaking scholars. The process of translation and assimilation was followed in the tenth and eleventh centuries by a creative phase of systematic philosophical, scientific and medical authorship, whose principal representatives were al-Kindī, al-Rāzi (d. c. 925), al-Fārābī, Avicenna and others.

Not only in the eastern parts of the Islamic caliphate, but also in the western parts, especially Muslim Spain (al-Andalus), learning began to gain momentum, and before long Cordova, the capital of Muslim Spain, began to vie with Baghdad as the center of learning. By the end of the eleventh century, eminent philosophers or physicians such as Avempace, Ibn Ṭufayl and Averroes began to appear on the cultural scene.

The significance of the Arab–Spanish phase in the development of Arab–Greek philosophy and science is that Iberia was the bridge across which Arab-Greek philosophy and science crossed into Western Europe, preparing the ground in due course for the rise of Latin Scholasticism, one of the glories of Western thought in the later Middle Ages, and subsequently the rise of the Renaissance in the fifteenth century.

Hebrew and Latin Translations of Averroes' Writings

The process of transmission took the form of translating Arabic scientific, medical and philosophical works into Hebrew or Latin, as early as the middle of the twelfth century. The earliest translations from Arabic tended to be medical or astronomical–astrological, such as Abū Ma'shar's introduction to astronomy, or *Introductorium in Astronomiam Albumasar,* translated around 1141, Dioscorides' *Materia Medica* and the medical corpus of Galen, the great Alexandrian physician and philosopher. Some of al-Fārābī's and Avicenna's philosophical works, together with parts of the latter's *Canon of Medicine,* were translated by a variety of scholars, such as John of Seville, Dominicus Jundissalinus and others. However, the star of this early translation movement was Gerard of Cremona (d. 1187) to whom no fewer than seventy medical, scientific and philosophical translations are attributed, including Aristotle's *Analytica Posteriora, De Coelo, De Generatione et Corruptione,* the pseudo-Aristotelian *Liber de Causis* and Avicenna's *Canon of Medicine.*[1]

However, the most important part of the Arab–Islamic philosophical legacy to find its way into Western Europe and to exert a lasting influence on Western-European thought, during the thirteenth century and beyond, was Averroes' corpus of Aristotelian commentaries. As mentioned earlier, Averroes had written three types of commentaries on the works of Aristotle, known as the large (*tafsīr*), intermediate (*sharh*) and short (paraphrases or summaries). The first type consisted of phrase-by-phrase commentaries on Aristotle's major treatises, the *Physics,* the *Metaphysics, De Coelo, Analytica Posteriora* and *De Anima,* on which Averroes wrote also intermediate and short commentaries or paraphrases (*jawāmi'*), which have all survived in Arabic or Hebrew and Latin translations.[2] In addition, Averroes wrote a paraphrase of Plato's *Republic* to serve as a substitute for Aristotle's *Politics,* which as we mentioned earlier, was not translated into Arabic until modern times.

---

1. Cf. Kretzmann *et al., The Cambridge History of Later Medieval Philosophy,* pp. 74 f. and Sarton, *Introduction to the History of Science II,* pp. 338f.
2. For a list of the commentaries, see Wolfson, "Revised Plan for Publication of a Corpus Averrois Commentariorum in Aristotelem", pp. 90 f.

The translation of Averroes' writings, especially his Aristotelian commentaries, was started by the Jews of Spain who were profoundly interested in Arabic philosophy. Rénan goes so far as to declare that "Arabic philosophy was never really taken seriously except by the Jews... whose literary culture in the Middle Ages is merely a reflection of Muslim culture."[3] The particular interest of the Jews in Averroes' writings stemmed from the high regard in which he was held by the great Jewish Aristotelian of Cordova, Moses Maimonides (d. 1204), who confesses in a letter addressed to his disciple, Joseph Ben Juda, written in Cairo in 1191, that "he had received lately everything Averroes had written on the works of Aristotle and found that he was extremely right, but had not had the time to study those writings."[4] The two Aristotelians had so much in common, especially in their attitude to Ash'arite *Kalām*, that readers of Maimonides tended to find Averroes particularly intriguing and to look upon the former as the disciple of the latter.

The first Jewish translator or paraphrast of Averroes' physical and metaphysical writings was Samuel Ben Tibbon, who based his *Opinions of the Philosophers* almost exclusively on Averroes. Other Jewish scholars, such as Juda Ben Solomon Cohen of Toledo, in his book the *Search for Wisdom*, and Shem Tob Ben Joseph Falquera, relied completely on Averroes, quoting him sometimes word by word.

The first Jewish translator of Averroes in the strict sense was Joseph Ben Abba Mari of Naples, who translated for Frederic II Averroes' commentaries on the *Organon* around 1232. Around 1260, Moses Ben Tibbon published an almost complete translation of Averroes' commentaries, as well as some of his medical writings. In 1259, Solomon Ben Joseph of Granada translated the commentary on *De Coelo et Mundo* and in 1284, Zerachia Ben Isaac of Barcelona translated the commentaries on the *Physics*, the *Metaphysics* and *De Coelo et Mundo*.

One of the most famous later Jewish translators of Averroes was Calonym Ben Calonym of Arles in France, who translated between 1314 and 1317 the commentaries on the *Topics*, the *Sophistica*, the *Analytica Posteriora*, the *Metaphysics*, the *Physics*, *De Coelo et Mundo*, *De Anima*, *On*

3. Rénan, *Averroes*, p. 173.
4. *Ibid.*, p. 177.

Generation and Corruption and the *Union of the Separate Intellect with Man*. In addition, Calonym made a Latin translation of Averroes' *Incoherence of the Incoherence* as *Destructio Destructionis* (*Tahāfut al-Tahāfut*) in 1328.[5]

The Jewish Averroist tradition reached its zenith in the fourteenth century and soon spread into France across the Pyrenees. Thus Rabbi Samuel Ben Juda Ben Meshullam of Marseilles translated in 1321 the commentary on the *Nicomachean Ethics* and the *Paraphrase of Plato's "Republic"*. Todros Todrosi of Arles translated in 1337 the commentaries on the *Topica, Sophistica, Rhetorica, Poetica* and *Ethica*.

The most famous Jewish philosopher of the fourteenth century, Levi Ben Gerson, commented on the various commentaries and other works of Averroes, such as *De Substantia orbis* and the *Possibility of the Union of the Separate Intellect with Man*, as did Moses of Narbonne, who commented extensively on the whole Averroist corpus. However, the best representative of Jewish Averroism, as such, was Elias Ben Medigo, who taught at Padua, which had become by the fourteenth century the center of Averroist studies. He wrote a commentary on Averroes' *De Substantia Orbis* and *Annotations on Averroes*. In the sixteenth century, Peripateticism and Averroism entered a period of recession, which heralded the dawn of modern thought and the growth of gradual anti-Aristotelian trends in European thought, as illustrated by the work of Michel de Montaigne (d. 1592), Francis Bacon (d. 1626), René Descartes (d. 1650), Nicolas de Malébranche (d. 1715) and others.

The Jewish translations paved the way for the Latin translations, sometimes collaterally, of Averroes' commentaries on Aristotle. Those translations which began early in the thirteenth century had a more durable impact on European thought and led at once to the rediscovery of Aristotle, who had been almost completely forgotten, as we have seen, in Western Europe, since the time of Boethius.

The first Latin translator of Averroes' commentaries was Michael the Scot (d. 136) who was responsible for translating, starting in 1217 at Toledo and Paris, the large commentaries on the *Physics*, the *Metaphysics*, *De Anima* and *De Coelo*, as well as the middle commentaries of *De*

5. *Ibid.*, p. 191.

Generatione et Corruptione, the *Meteorologica,* IV and the epitomes of *De Coelo, Parva Naturalia* and *De Animalibus.* Shortly after, Hermann the German (d. 1272) translated at Toledo the middle commentaries on the *Nicomachean Ethics* and the *Poetics;* while William de Luna translated the middle commentaries on Porphyry's *Isagoge,* Aristotle's *Categories, De Interpretatione, Analytica Priora* and *Posteriora.*[6] Averroes' medical treatise, *al-Kulliyāt,* was translated as *Colliget* in the middle of the thirteenth century by an anonymous translator. The commentary on the medical poem (*al-Urjūzah*) of Avicenna was translated by Armengaud, son of Blaise of Montpellier, where some of Averroes' medical tracts were translated by a number of Latin scholars, assisted by Jewish colleagues.

As Latin versions of Averroes' commentaries began to circulate in Scholastic circles, they were met with opposition from such theologians as William of Auvergne, Albert the Great and others. Albert the Great, the teacher of St. Thomas Aquinas, was an admirer of Avicenna, which would explain in part his opposition to Averroes. What both William and Albert objected to in Averroes' teaching or interpretation of Aristotle was the theory of the unity of the intellect, of which St. Thomas was the chief critic, as the next chapter will show in some detail. This interpretation, William and Albert argued, militated against the concept of personal responsibility or initiative and hampered the process of personal intellection.

Latin Averroism in Paris and Padua

Before long, however, there grew around Averroes' name a large and determined circle of followers, first at Paris and subsequently at Padua and elsewhere in Italy, known as Latin Averroists. Their leaders in Paris were Siger of Brabant (d. 1281) and Boethius of Dacia (d. 1284), whose influence in theological circles was such that the church authorities at Paris felt compelled to intervene. Thus, in 1270, Etienne Tempier, Bishop of Paris, issued a condemnation of fifteen propositions which were in conflict with Catholic doctrine, according to him. They included the denial of divine providence, the view that the will was a passive, not an

6. Kretzmann *et al., The Cambridge History,* pp. 48 f. and Rénan, *Averroès,* pp. 205 f.

active faculty of the soul, which is necessarily determined by desire, the eternity of the world and the primacy of philosophical over religious truth. Most of these propositions were believed to follow from Aristotle's teaching or Averroes' interpretation. In 1277, a papal bull was issued on which Etienne Tempier based his second condemnation of 219 theses directed against Averroes, Aristotle and their followers at the University of Paris, but did not spare St. Thomas himself.[7]

The two condemnations weakened Parisian Averroism, as did St. Thomas' sustained critique of the three principal issues of the eternity of the world, the unity of the intellect and the scope of divine providence. However, Averroism continued to gain ground in Italy, especially at Padua. The great Florentine poet, Dante Alighieri (d. 1321), himself based upon Averroes' theory of the possible intellect a whole new secularist theory of the state in his *De Monarchia*. This theory was intended as a challenge of the Papal claim that the emperor receives his authority from 'the Vicar of Christ' or Pope, rather than directly from God. In the *De Monarchia*, which was written in Latin and reveals a vast philosophical erudition, Dante argues along Averroist lines that man's essence consists "in the capacity to apprehend by means of the possible intellect; and it is this which sets him apart from inferior and superior beings."[8] For as he hastens to explain, inferior beings or brutes do apprehend in some sense, and superior beings or angels are endowed with an intellect, which is not possible, like mankind, but rather fully actual.

From the unity of the possible intellect, in which all mankind share, Dante goes on to draw the logical inference that mankind is politically one. For the "task proper to mankind, considered as a whole," he writes, "is to fulfill the total capacity of the possible intellect all the time, primarily by speculation and secondarily as a function of speculation, by action."[9] The fulfillment of this double task is incumbent on man as an individual, Dante argues, and humanity, as a single community, seeking to achieve the highest goals to which it is destined to strive; namely, universal peace and terrestrial happiness.

7. Cf. Mandonnet, *Siger de Brabant*, pt. 1, p. 111, and pt. 2, p. 178.
8. *Monarchy and Three Political Letters*, p. 7.
9. *Ibid.*, p. 8.

This reliance on the authority of Averroes, to whom Dante has referred in the *Divine Comedy* as '*che gran commento feo*,' in recognition of his contribution as the Commentator of Aristotle, exposed Dante shortly after his death to the then serious charge of Averroism. In 1327, he was publicly accused of Averroism by a Dominican scholar, Guido Vernani, and *De Monarchia* was burnt in the market-place of Bologna by order of Pope John XXII.

During the first half of the fourteenth century, the leading Italian teachers at Padua carried the torch of Averroism, whether in philosophy or medicine. Those teachers included Gregory of Rimini, Jerome Ferrari, Fra Urbano of Bologna, Marsilius of Padua, John of Jandun and Pierre of Abano. John of Jandun (d. 1328) was the most famous of those teachers and the one who had for Averroes the highest regard as '*perfectissimus et gloriosissimus physicus, veritates amicus et defensor entrepidus*' (the most perfect and glorious physician, friend and fearless defender of the truth).[10] As a thoroughgoing Averroist, John of Jandun upheld the eternity of the world, the unity of the intellect and the impossibility of personal immortality, on philosophical grounds, in an unqualified manner. On the question of creation *ex nihilo*, which was at the center of the Averroist controversy, he took the position that it was philosophically indemonstrable and untenable. "I say," he wrote, "that God can do it; how, I do not know; God only knows."[11] As a good Latin Averroist, however, he continued to adhere to this and similar propositions on the ground of faith, rather than reason, but clearly without much conviction.

The friend and close associate of Jean of Jandun, Marsilius of Padua (d. 1343), published in 1324 jointly with Jean a famous political treatise entitled *Defensor Pacis* (Defender of Peace) with profound Averroist undertones. In this treatise, Marsilius defends the thesis of the separation of reason and faith, at the philosophical level, and that of the church and state, at the political level – a thesis which was thought to follow from the teaching of Averroes. For Marsilius, religious truths cannot be demonstrated by reason, but are not on that account wrong or questionable. For as Averroes had actually taught, religion plays an important moral and

10. Rénan, *Averroès*, p. 341.
11. Gilson, *La philosophie au moyen âge*, p. 689.

social role in ensuring the harmony and stability of the social order, by instilling in the souls of the citizens the practical virtues. Jointly with the theoretical virtues, these practical virtues are the warrant of man's happiness in this world.

It can thus be seen how the secularist thesis, defended by both Dante and Marsilius of Padua, who based it explicitly on Averroes' teaching, marked the dawn of a new phase in European political thought. This new secularist phase rested ultimately on the concept of the primacy and autonomy of reason, which both in its 'possible' and active capacity, as Averroes had taught, was truly universal. This concept marked, in addition, the dawn of that rationalism and humanism which the Italian Renaissance first preached, but which culminated in the 'mathematical rationalism' of René Descartes, generally regarded as the father of modern philosophy. What sets Averroes' 'philosophical rationalism' apart is its comprehensive character, since it was not limited to the Cartesian reasoning *more geometrico.*

Although John of Jandun and Marsilius of Padua were the stars of Italian Averroism, there were many others, such as Urbano of Bologna, Paul of Venice, Paul of Pergola, John of Lendinare and Nicholas of Foligno, who are listed by Rénan as leading Averroist masters in the fourteenth century.[12]

Other Italian masters, such as Gaetano of Tiene, Michael Savonarola and Pietro Pompanazzi (d. 1525), continued the Averroist tradition at Padua, Bologna and elsewhere into the fifteenth century. Pompanazzi was the first scholar to break publicly, in his interpretation of Aristotle, with Averroes in favor of Alexander of Aphrodisias, but as Rénan has put it: "If we apply the name Averroist to this family of thinkers who were troubled and exasperated by [religious] constraints, so numerous in Italy during the Renaissance, and who hid behind the name of the Commentator [i.e. Averroes], Pompanazzi must be placed in the forefront of Averroists."[13]

Like Averroes, Pompanazzi tended to relegate religion to the purely practical domain of controlling the masses and ensuring the stability of the social order. Religious doctrines, for him, do contain a certain measure

12. Rénan, *Averroès,* pp. 346 f.
13. *Ibid.,* p. 360.

of truth, in so far as they can serve the pragmatic purpose of persuading the masses to act in conformity with the prescriptions stemming from those doctrines, and to lead a life of moral virtue.[14]

The leading Averroists of the sixteenth century included Nicoletti Vernias, Niphus, Achillini and Zimara. Niphus and Zimara were the most accomplished commentators on the works of Averroes and Aristotle, and despite ecclesiastical reservations or protestations, it is significant that Averroes remained for those scholars the most authoritative interpreter of Aristotle, "the Master of all those who know," as Dante had put it in the *Divine Comedy*, as distinct from Averroes, the *Commentator.*

14. Pine, *Pietro Pompanazzi*, p. 34.

11

Averroes and Aquinas

Reconciliation of Reason and Faith

As the two greatest Aristotelians of the twelfth and thirteenth centuries, Averroes and Aquinas, had, despite their differences, a great deal in common. Apart from writing the most elaborate commentaries, prior to modern times, on the works of Aristotle, they were both genuinely interested in reconciling his metaphysical and ethical teaching with religious orthodoxy, Islamic in the first case and Christian in the second. In addition, they were both profoundly interested in a series of philosophical–theological questions, including the relation of reason and faith, human liberty and divine providence, the demonstrability of God's existence and His attributes, the creation of the world, the immortality of the soul and the resurrection of the body. Thus, as we have seen, Averroes wrote one of the most systematic treatises in Arabic on the relation of reason and revelation, or philosophy and religion, entitled the *Decisive Treatise on the Relation of Philosophy and Reason,* in which he dealt with this question in a manner thoroughly comparable to Aquinas' procedure in the opening parts of the *Summa Theologica* (Prima Pars) and his other works. More specifically, in the other theological treatise, the *Exposition of the Methods of Proof,* Averroes' discussion of God's existence, His attributes, His creation of the world, free will and predestination is reminiscent of Aquinas' own discussion of these questions in his various scholastic writings.[1] The striking correspondence between their two methods of dealing with this common cluster of questions was not purely coincidental; it stemmed from the common philosophical legacy they had both inherited, and whose ultimate source was Aristotelianism, as applied to the Qur'an in the one case or the Bible in the other. Strangely, the two just-mentioned treatises of Averroes were never translated into Latin, even at the height of the Latin Averroist triumph in the Western world.

Nevertheless, the reception of Averroes by the Latin theologians and philosophers of the thirteenth and fourteenth centuries, as we have seen, was mixed; and although he had a large and enthusiastic following at Paris, Padua and elsewhere, he soon met with staunch opposition from both philosophical and ecclesiastical quarters.

The standard-bearer of Latin Averroism in Paris, as we have seen, was Siger of Brabant, who, before long, came into conflict with the greatest Aristotelian of his day, St. Thomas Aquinas, who dissociated himself from the Averroist interpretation of Aristotle on such questions as the eternity of the world *ex nihilo* and the scope of divine providence. Significantly enough, he was in perfect agreement with him on the questions of essence and existence, contingency and necessity and secondary causality, repudiated by Avicenna and the Ash'arites. It may be appropriate, therefore, to close the present study with a systematic exposition of the stand of both philosophers on these and related questions.

'On Being and Essence'

We might begin with the question of essence and existence, or *De Ente et Essentia*, which was the title of one of Aquinas' earliest works, written before March 1256, when he became Master of Theology at the University of Paris.[2]

In this carefully written treatise, St. Thomas attempts to pinpoint the distinction between a cluster of Aristotelian terms, being (*ens*), essence (*essentia, quiditas*), matter, form, genus, species, differentia and substance

1. See, for instance, *Summa Theologica* I, Questions 2, 3, 5, 6, 22, 44, 82, etc.
2. See *On Being and Essence*, p. 8.

(*ousia*). In some respects, the *De Ente et Essentia* may be regarded as a logical treatise, due to Aquinas' preoccupation with the analysis of these terms. A noteworthy feature of this analysis is the explicit dependence of its author on Avicenna and Averroes, whose works had become available to Latin scholars by this time, on the one hand, and his use of a key term, *esse*, for which there was really no equivalent in Greek or Arabic, on the other.[3] This term, borrowed probably from Boethius, became in Aquinas' maturer works the pivotal metaphysical term and is applied in the first instance to God, who is stated in *Summa Theologica* I, Q. 3, a. 4, and Q. 44, a. 1, to be *esse per se subsistens*; since in Him alone is the unity of essence and existence safeguarded. Based originally on Avicenna's account in *Metaphysics*, to which Aquinas repeatedly refers in *De Ente et Essentia*, the concept of the unity of essence and existence in God is deepened in a variety of ways. First, Aquinas denies Avicenna's claim that, for the above-mentioned reason, God has no essence.[4] Secondly, he invokes the authority of Aristotle and that of the Commentator (Averroes) to assert that, unlike all other entities, whether physical or intellectual, God possesses all the perfections "in a more excellent way" (*modus eminenter*) than all other things, because in Him they are one; whereas in other things they are diversified. For unlike all other entities, these perfections belong to Him in virtue of His simple being, which is identified with His essence.[5]

Apart from this application of the concept of perfection to God and the creatures analogically, divergence from Avicenna in his conception of being is best gauged if we set it against Averroes' vehement critique of the latter's view of being as an accident, which supervenes upon essence and brings it thereby into existence. To God, to whom Avicenna refers as the Necessary Being, existence belongs essentially; whereas all other entities, being contingent or possible (*jā'iz*, or *mumkin*) in themselves, may be described as 'necessary through another,' i.e., the Necessary Being, who is their ultimate cause.

---

3. A possible exception in Greek may be Parmenides, the Eleatic philosopher, who opens his poem *On Truth* by stating that only *estin einai*, or to be, is, and *ouk estin* is not.
4. Cf. *On Being and Essence*, p. 60.
5. *Ibid.*, p. 62. Aquinas is referring in this connection to Aristotle's *Metaphysics* V, 1021b 30, and to Averroes' *In Metaphysicoprum* V, f.c. 21, fol. 62r. 10–13.

Averroes begins by scoffing at the notion of a being (the world) which is contingent in itself, but becomes necessary through another, as a patently self-contradictory notion. He then proceeds to accuse Avicenna and the Ash'arites of subscribing to a view of the universe as contingent on purely "dialectical and untrue grounds." For, according to him, once we posit the series of natural and supernatural causes which operate upon existing entities in the world as a whole, their mode of being, forms and properties would cease to be contingent and become necessary instead. Such, in fact, is the character of the universe as a whole. If we deny this, we would be forced to deny the wisdom of the Creator, and then we would have no ground for rebutting the views of those who believe in a random creation. We will also be unable to prove the existence of the Wise Maker (*Sāni'*) of the world, as we have seen in an earlier chapter.

Later, we will return to the general metaphysical and theological strictures of both Averroes and Aquinas, against the Avicennian concept of contingency and the parallel Ash'arite repudiation of 'secondary' causality. Suffice it to note at this stage that for Averroes the necessity (*wujūb*) which attaches to the creation is a logical corollary of the wisdom and goodness of God, who did not abandon the world to the vagaries of chance (*ittifāq*), as the Materialists have done.[6]

Averroes goes on, as we saw in an earlier chapter, to accuse Avicenna of confusing the meaning of being as existing, with that of being as one; i.e., the ontological and numerical meanings (recognized by Aristotle); and having observed that the latter is an accident, he was led to the false conclusion that being is an accident, too. In the same manner, having confused the being which denotes genus with that which denotes the true, admittedly an accident, Avicenna was mistakenly led, likewise, to conclude that being is an accident.[7]

St. Thomas, in distinct Aristotelian and Averroist fashion, rejects this Avicennian notion of the accidentality of being, on the ground that existing entities, as effects of the creative power of God who is self-subsisting being (*esse per se subsistens*), must possess being essentially, rather than accidentally.

6. Cf. *al-Kashf*, pp. 154 and 201 f.
7. Aristotle, in *Metaphysics* V, 1017a 32, identifies being with the true and in *Metaphysics* XI, 1061a 15, he regards being and one as convertible terms.

Moreover, in so far as they 'are not their own being' and their existence is not identical with their essence, as is the case with God alone, such effects may be said to exist by participation, and as such must derive their existence from God, or "the One First Being, who possesses being most perfectly."[8] The act of creation is then described by him as the process whereby God brings what is in potentiality into a state of actuality, and thus being is stated to be to essence what actuality is to potentiality. Hence, he writes: "Being is the actuality of every form or nature... Therefore, being must be compared to essence, if the latter is distinct from it, as actuality to potentiality,"[9] or as he has put it more explicitly elsewhere: "Being is the actuality of every act and thus is the perfection of every perfection."[10]

From this last statement, it is clear how thoroughly Aristotelian was Aquinas' concept of the relation of being to essence and how far removed it was from Avicenna's. If existence or being is identified with actuality, then any implication of its being accidental or even 'happening,' in Avicenna's sense, would be excluded, and the defense of the latter against the charge of the accidentality of being, which some scholars have recently attempted, entirely futile. The existing entity (*mawjūd*), does not 'happen' to come into being and cannot be said to be generated through a process of becoming or change. This Aristotle had denied on the ground that generation is not a form of motion or change, but an act *sui generis*,[11] for the entity is produced or created at once and creation can only be described as an act of the Creator. In relation to its essence or form, which is universal, it is undoubtedly particular or individual. Therefore, its coming-to-be through creation cannot be described as an accident, in any sense of that word. On the contrary, being, in the Aristotelian–Thomist view, is the very essence of the existing entity. Avicenna's starting-point was clearly Platonic, although he was struggling unsuccessfully to fit the theory of essences into an Aristotelian framework.[12]

8. *Summa Theologica* I, Q. 44, a. 1. Cf. Q. 3, a. 3 and a. 4.

9. *Ibid.*, I, Q. 3, a. 4.

10. *Quest. Disp. de Anima*, Q. 7, a. 2 and 9. Cf. Gilson, *Being and Some Philosophers*, p. 175.

11. *De Gen. et Corrup.* I, 317b 6 f. and *Physics* V, 225a 20 f.

12. See Rahman, "Essence and Existence in Avicenna," *Medieval and Renaissance Studies*, pp. 1–16; and Burrel, "Aquinas's Attitude towards Avicenna, Maimonides and Averroes," *The Cambridge Companion to Aquinas*, pp. 69 f., for a defense of Avicenna. For Avicenna's view, see *al-Ishārāt wa'l-Tanbihât*, pp. 144 f.

Aristotle had, in *Metaphysics* IV, 10506b 1 and elsewhere, identified substance with actuality, which he regarded as prior to potentiality. By substance (*ousia*), in the primary sense, he meant being. For, as he writes in a memorable passage (*Met.* VII, 1028b 1f.): "Indeed the question which was raised of old and is raised now and always; and is always the subject of doubt, viz., what being is, is just the question, What is substance?"

Actuality is thus the hallmark of being, not only regarding existing entities or individual substances, but also regarding God, or the Unmoved Mover. Thus in *Metaphysics* XII, 1072b 25, Aristotle describes the Unmoved Mover as eternal substance (*ousia*) and actuality (*energeia*), which he then proceeds to identify with life. By life, according to him, should be understood the actuality of thought; so that God, who is thought thinking itself, should be regarded as the actuality of thought or life 'most good and eternal.'

In his discussion of the origination (*ījād*) of the world, Averroes interprets Aristotle to mean that the process of origination is simply a matter of combining potentiality and actuality, matter and form, or bringing them together, as we have seen earlier. This process, he explains, is entirely different from bringing the effect out of nothing, as Muslim and Christian theologians hold.[13]

The Avicennian concept of contingency and the parallel Ash'arite repudiation of secondary causality were at the center of the classic controversy between Muslim theologians and Aristotelians, from the tenth century on. Al-Ghazālī, as we have seen, was the standard-bearer of the anti-Aristotelian party, who had, in his *Tahāfut al-Falāsifah* and elsewhere, stripped all created entities of any causal efficacy and referred every mode of activity in the world to the direct and constant intervention of God, who was for him the Sole Agent. This view, generally designated as occasionalism because of its similarity to the view of Descartes' most famous disciple, Malébranche, became, almost from the tenth century onward, the official doctrine of Muslim theologians in general and Ash'arites in particular.[14]

---

13. *Tafsīr* III, pp. 1497 f. Cf. *Tahāfut al-Tahāfut*, p. 180 f.
14. Cf. Fakhry, *History of Islamic Philosophy*, pp. 209 f., and *Islamic Occasionalism*, passim.

The two greatest critics of occasionalism, in the name of Arisotelian-
ism, were Averroes in the twelth century and St. Thomas Aquinas in the
thirteenth. In the case of Averroes, the dialectical battle was joined under
the banner of rationalism. In his rebuttal of al-Ghazālī's *Tahāfut al-
Falāsifah,* Averroes bluntly states that "Whoever repudiates causality," as
the Ash'arites have done, "simply repudiates reason."[15] In the case of
Aquinas, it was joined under the banner of divine providence and the way
in which belief in an omnipotent and sovereign Creator and Ruler of the
world does not necessarily contradict the belief in a causally ordered
universe.

Rehabilitation of Causality

The rehabilitation of Aristotle, which Averroes undertook, stipulated that
the causal efficacy of the created order be salvaged and the alleged
contingency of the world and its components, upheld by Avicenna, be
rejected.

It will be recalled that in his *Tahāfut,* al-Ghazālī rejected the causal
nexus on two grounds: theological and epistemological. On the first
ground, he argues that belief in a necessary causal sequence of events in
the world militates against the Qur'anic concept of God's unlimited power
and His prerogative to act miraculously in the world, "in which Muslims
unanimously concur."[16] On the second ground, he argues that the alleged
correlation between so-called effects and so-called causes is not
necessary; it is neither borne out by sense-experience (*mushāhadah*) nor
by logical reasoning. It is simply a matter of habit, born of the constant
recurrence of observable cause–effect sequences, as David Hume was to
argue in the eighteenth century. For, in the first place, sense-experience
does not bear out the claim of the philosophers that the effect happens
through the cause (*bi hī*) but simply with it (*ma'ahu*). In the second place,
logical reasoning does not bear out the claim of the necessary correlation
between causes and effects either, but rather contradicts it. For to attribute
causal efficacy to inanimate objects (*jamād*), such as burning to fire, is

15. *Tahāfut al-Tahāfut,* p. 520.
16. *Tahāfut al-Falāsifah,* p. 276. Cf. Supra.

rationally unwarranted, in so far as efficacy (*fi'l*) is a prerogative of animate agents only. If so, it follows that all activity must be referred to God, either indirectly through the angels or directly, since "He is the Lord of Lords and the Cause of Causes." He is the only Agent besides whom there is no other agent.[17]

In his rebuttal, Averroes, as we have seen, begins by rejecting the claim that belief in the necessary correlation between causes and effects is a matter of habit (*'ādah*), on the ground that the concept of habit is ambiguous. The Ash'arites might mean by habit that of the natural agent, that of God or that of the human observer. In the first instance, it is absurd to attribute habit to God whose "ways are immutable" as the Qur'an (35:42) has put it. In the second instance, habit can only refer to our ability, as human observers, to judge of things as they are. In that sense, "habit is nothing other than the action of reason, as stipulated by its very nature, whereby it is called reason."[18] In fact, Averroes goes on: "reason is nothing other than the causal apprehension of existing entities," as Aristotle had actually asserted in defining scientific knowledge (*episteme*) in *Analytica Posteriora* I, 71a 10 f. and elsewhere.

Moreover, al-Ghazālī and the Ash'arites, by denying the necessary connections between events, have repudiated the divine wisdom exhibited in the rational order pertaining to God's workmanship, and thereby have repudiated the possibility of demonstrating the existence of God from the beauty and order exhibited in this workmanship. Such a position is not only incompatible with the teaching of the philosophers, but also runs counter to the express pronouncements of the Qur'an, which exhorts the believers repeatedly to "ponder" or "reflect upon" God's multifarious creation (78:6 f.) and the rational order he has imparted to it (7:184).[19]

It was primarily for this reason that Averroes favored the two arguments of divine providence (*dalīl al-'ināyah*) and invention (*ikhtirā'*), for the existence of God, "to which the precious Book [i.e., the Qur'an] has drawn attention and has exhorted us all to follow," as we have seen earlier.

17. *Ibid.*, pp. 131 and 295.
18. *Tahāfut al-Tahāfut*, p. 520.
19. Cf. *al-Kashf*, pp. 151 f.

Aquinas's Critique of Ash'arite Occasionalism

It is also in the context of divine providence that St. Thomas launches his attack against the Muslim (Ash'arite) theologians, to whom he refers as the *Loquentes in lege Maurorum* in the *Summa Contra Gentiles* and elsewhere.

In his discussion of divine providence, he begins by observing that, whether we believe the world to have come into being by emanation (as the Neoplatonists have held), or by creation as Faith stipulates, things are preserved in existence by God, who is thus both the Creator and the Preserver of the world. In support of this thesis he quotes St. Paul (Heb. 1: 3) and St. Augustine (4 Super Gen. Ad. Lit. XII) and then proceeds to assert: "Hereby is refuted the statement of certain authorities quoted in the law of the Moors, who, in order to be able to maintain that the world needs to be preserved by God, held that all forms are accidents, and that no accident lasts for two instants."[20] Relying on Maimonides' *Guide of the Perplexed* (*Dux Perplexorum*), St. Thomas then goes on to discuss the Ash'arites' view that all substances are made up of indivisible bodies (i.e., atoms), in which the transient accidents inhere. Some of those accidents, however, have a certain measure of permanence, but do not cease to exist, according to some of those theologians, unless God creates in them the accident of cessation. Here, St. Thomas is clearly referring to Maimonides' account in the *Guide* (Prop. 6), where he comments on the views of those Mutakallimun, who believed that the permanence or durability of bodies, made up of atoms and accidents, depends on God's decision to keep them in existence. Should He decide, contrariwise, to destroy these bodies, He would be compelled to create the 'accident of cessation' (*fanā*) in them, according to some of the Mutakallimun, or to create the accident of cessation in no substratum, according to others, whereupon the world would cease at once to exist.[21]

In criticizing this 'occasionalist' view, St. Thomas observes that all power is ultimately derived from God, who is the First Cause of being, as well as of perfection. This divine power, however, is mediated by

20. *S. Cont. Gent.* III, ch. 65.
21. Cf. *Dalalat* I, 73, pp. 201 f. (Pines, pp. 200 f.) The first view is attributed to the Ash'arite al-Qalanisi by al-Baghdadi, *Usūl al-Din*, p. 62; the second to the Mu'tazilite al-Jubā'i and his son, Abū Hashim. Cf. al-Ash'ari, *Maqālat al-Islamiyin*, p. 366.

secondary agents, whether physical or human, who share in God's power, as they share in His being. Accordingly, to strip created entities of their power is to derogate from the perfection or power of God.[22]

Not only the Ash'arites, but also the Jewish philosopher Avicebron (Ibn Gebirol) (d. 1070), are accused of subscribing to this view, which may be called the 'inertness' of created substances. The Ash'arites justified this view, as we have seen, on the ground that activity cannot be attributed to these substances, since it is the exclusive prerogative of God. Avicebron, on the other hand, justified it on the ground that corporeal substance, being the farthest removed from God, the only active Agent, is devoid of any causal efficacy.[23]

St. Thomas refers to another argument of the Ash'arites in support of their view of the total inertness of corporeal substances; namely, that the accidents entering into their composition cannot pass from one subject to another. Accordingly, no object can be said to operate on any other object and God must constantly create the accident or accidents in question, first in the body designated as the agent, and next in the body designated as the patient. Thus, heat cannot pass from one object to another, but must first be created by God in the body which is the cause of heating, and subsequently in the body which is the effect or recipient of the heating process.[24] In criticizing this thesis of the inertness of corporeal substance, St. Thomas first observes that it is contrary to divine wisdom. For, if creatures do not produce any effects and God alone is responsible for their production, entities which appear to us to operate on their objects would have been created in vain. Moreover, the perfection of the effect is a token of the perfection of its cause. Now, if we rob created entities of any causal efficacy, we would have detracted from their perfection, and by extension from the perfection of their Maker. For, "It is due to the abundance of its perfection," St. Thomas writes, "that a thing is able to communicate to another the perfection that it has."[25] This same criticism can be expressed in another way. It belongs to God, as the Supreme Good,

22. *S. Cont. Gent.* III, ch. 67.
23. *Ibid.*, ch. 69, where St. Thomas appears to be referring to Avicebron's *Fons Vitae*, tract II, III.
24. Cf. *S. Cont. Gent.* III, ch. 69, and Maimonides, *Guide* I, 73 prop. 6.
25. *Ibid.*, ch. 69.

to impart to created entities the power to communicate their goodness to other entities by means of their transitive operations. Therefore, God communicates His goodness by empowering His creatures to communicate to other things the goodness that He originally imparted to them.

A third criticism of the view of the inertness of created entities is that it amounts to robbing the world of that order which only the interaction of its parts can generate. By robbing created entities of their active powers, we would be robbing them of the ability to contribute to that universal order which God has imparted to His creation, as St. Thomas has put it.[26]

Like Aristotle and Averroes, St. Thomas next argues that the nature of the cause can only be inferred from the power exhibited in the effect. Therefore, if we deny the power of creatures to produce certain effects, "it will follow that the nature of a creature can never be known from its effect, so that all the knowledge of physical science would be denied us; for it is there that arguments from effects are chiefly employed."[27] Aristotle, in fact, went even further and defined wisdom (*sophia*), the highest mode of knowledge, as knowledge of certain principles and causes, and 'first philosophy,' or metaphysics, as the knowledge of *first* principles and causes.[28] In *Analytica Posteriora* I, 71b 10, he defines scientific knowledge (*episteme*), in general, as the knowledge of "the cause on which the fact depends, as the cause of that fact and no other, and further, that the fact could not be other than it is." In other words, such knowledge must rest upon the specific knowledge of the cause of the fact in question and must be necessary.

And finally, to refute the thesis of the Ash'arites that bodies cannot act on other bodies, because accidents cannot be transmitted from one body to another, St. Thomas adduces another argument. When a certain body is said to act on another body, causing it, for instance, to become hot, it is not the case that the identical property or form, in this case heat, passes from the first body to the second. But instead, the form or property inherent in the object upon which the natural agent acts is reduced from a state of

26. *S. Cont. Gent.* III, ch. 69.
27. Cf. *S. Cont. Gent.* III, ch. 69.
28. *Metaphysics* I, 981b 30 f.

potentiality to a state of actuality. The recipient or patient, originally potentially hot, now becomes actually hot.[29] Thus, the spatial language of transmission (*intiqāl*), according to this interpretation, should be replaced by the metaphysical language of potentiality and actuality, in which Averroes, too, had expressed the concept of action, even when predicated of God Himself, as already mentioned.

It is to be noted at this point that the correspondence of the views of Averroes and Aquinas, regarding the accidentality of being and the contingency of the universe, upheld by Avicenna, on the one hand, and the occasionalism and explicit repudiation of causality by the Ash'arites, on the other, was not purely coincidental. As the two great heirs of the Aristotelian tradition, those two philosophers had a great deal in common. Ernest Rénan in his outstanding book, *Averroès et l'averroïsme*, first published in 1852, has put the peculiar relation of Averroes and Aquinas in these words: "St. Thomas (Aquinas) is the most serious adversary the Averroist doctrine has encountered; but we might state, without sounding paradoxical, that he is also the first disciple of the Great Commentator. Albert [the Great] owes all to Avicenna; St. Thomas, as a philosopher, owes all to Averroes."[30]

Rénan's nineteenth-century reference to St. Thomas' debt to Averroes has been reaffirmed by Edward Booth in his well-documented *Aristotelian Aporetic Ontology in Islamic and Christian Thinkers*, where he writes:

> The ontology of Ibn Rushd (Averroes) was, therefore, a greater tributary to the comprehensive ontological figure of Thomas than appears from the explicit references, and the critical association of Avicennian and Averroian theses in the *De Ente et Essentia* shows this to have been the case from his earlier writings.[31]

It is abundantly clear, we believe, that in his writings, St. Thomas moved progressively away from Avicennianism, with its deep grounding in Neoplatonism, with which he was never in sympathy. As an Aristotelian, St. Thomas must have felt a far greater affinity with the *Commentator* of the

29. *S. Cont. Gent.* III, ch. 69.
30. *Averroès*, p. 236.
31. Booth, *Aristotelian Aporetic Ontology*, p. 254.

'Prince of Philosophers' whose epistemology and ontology formed the cornerstone of his own philosophy.

However, it is an illusion to think that St. Thomas was in total agreement with Averroes in their respective interpretations of Aristotle. Perhaps, the most notorious instance of their divergence concerned the unity of the intellect, targeted in one of his well-known treatises, *De Unitate Intellectus, Contra Averroistas*. In this treatise, written in 1270 in Paris, St. Thomas marshals a whole array of arguments against the Averroist thesis of the unity or separability of the 'possible' intellect, i.e., the potential or material, known in Arabic as *hayūlāni*, or hylic. He begins by examining Aristotle's words in *De Anima* II and III, quoting Themistius' Commentary on the Soul, and referring to Theophrastus' view, as cited by Themistius and Alexander, as reported by Averroes in his *Large Commentary on the Soul*, which has survived only in Latin translation.[32] He then reviews the various statements of Averroes and those of the above-mentioned Greek commentators quoted by him, and finally concludes:

> The claim that the intellect is some principle separated in substance and yet is perfected and comes actually to understand through the species taken from phantasms [as Averroes actually held] is, therefore, improbable in the extreme to me.[33]

By the same token, St. Thomas, relying on his own reading of Aristotle's texts in *De Anima* and elsewhere, rejects the Averroist thesis of a single, universal possible intellect and quotes in support of his view Avicenna and Algazel (as al-Ghazālī was known in Latin circles), who vindicated the plurality of intellects. Here he writes:

> They speak falsehood who say that it was a principle with all those who philosophize, both Arabs and Peripatetics, if not for the Latins, that the intellect is not multiplied numerically. Algazel was an Arab, not a Latin.[34]

32. See *Averrois Cordubensis Commentarium Magnum*, p. 101.
33. *Aquinas Against the Averroists*, p. 101.
34. *Ibid.*, p. 139. St. Thomas quotes here Avicenna's *De Anima* III, 16–20. The Algazel referred to above is the author of the *Intentions of the Philosophers* (*Maqāsid al-Falāsifah*), known in Latin as *Philosophia et Logica Algazelis Arabes*, written originally as a prelude to his assault on Aristotelian philosophy, as represented by al-Fārābī and Avicenna, in the *Incoherence of the Philosophers*.

He then quotes a passage from Avicenna's *De Anima*, which states that "prudence, stupidity, opinion and other attributes of that sort can only inhere in the essence of the soul. Therefore, the soul is not numerically one, but many, though of one species."[35]

Now, if the possible intellect is not separable and is not one, it follows according to St. Thomas, commenting on *De Anima* III, 414b 18, that Aristotle believed "that the intellect is a power of the soul, which is the act of the body (*vult* [namely Aristotle] *ergo quod intellectus est potentia animae que est actus corporis*").[36] In this way, he rescues Aristotle from those interpretations, including Averroes', according to which the power of intellection lies outside the soul or body, as the thesis of one, separate possible intellect, common to the whole of mankind, clearly entails.

But was the Active Intellect, as its counterpart, one and separable, as Aristotle appears to imply in his famous statement in the *De Anima* III, 430a 16, "that mind in this sense of it, is separable (*choristos*), impassible (*apathis*) and unmixed (*amigis*)," or not?

Now, whether the Active Intellect, identified with God, as Alexander held, or with the last of those separate intelligences which emanate from the One or the Necessary Being, as Avicenna held, is one or multiple, raises the same cluster of questions as the possible intellect. St. Thomas pursues this issue relentlessly in *De Unitate Intellectus*, as well as in the *Summa Theologica*, the *Summa Contra Gentiles*, and elsewhere. His chief gambit is to probe the texts of Aristotle, with a view to demonstrating that, like the possible intellect, the Active Intellect is a power of the soul.

Aristotle, we might mention, had remained so ambivalent on this point that even today his interpreters are by no means unanimous. In the *Summa Theologica*, St. Thomas begins by asking whether there is such a thing as the Active (or agent) Intellect, which he answers in the affirmative. The reason he gives is extremely suggestive. For Plato, he says, there was no need to posit an Active Intellect, because Plato believed the forms of things (that is, the Ideas) which existed in the intelligible world, were already actual; and they are known by virtue of the fact that "our intellect was formed by participation (in these Ideas) in order to have knowledge of

---

35. *Aquinas Against the Averroists*, p. 139.
36. *Ibid.*, pp. 32–33. Cf. p. 69.

the genera and species of things."[37] Aristotle, on the other hand, denied the separate existence of the Ideas or forms apart from matter; therefore, he was led to posit an Active Intellect which reduced those forms from potentiality to actuality, through the process of abstraction, whereby they become actually intelligible, or fit objects of human cognition. That is why, according to St. Thomas, Aristotle compares the Active Intellect to light,[38] whereas Plato had compared it to the sun.[39]

Next, St. Thomas asks whether this Active Intellect is in the soul, or whether as Avicenna and Averroes had held, it is separate. Referring to a famous passage in *De Anima*, which states that, "since in every class of things, we find two factors involved, (1) a matter which is potentially all the particulars included in the class, (2) a cause which is productive in the sense that it makes them all . . . these distinct elements must likewise be found within the soul."[40] St. Thomas maintains that the Active Intellect exists in the soul. It is then characterized as "a superior intellect, from which the soul acquires the power of understanding," due to the fact that in itself the soul is imperfect, changeable and acquires knowledge by participation. "For what is such by participation, and what is movable [i.e., changeable] and what is imperfect, always requires the pre-existence of something essentially such, immovable and perfect."[41] He then refers to the views of those philosophers, who, like Alexander and Averroes, believed that the soul's knowledge, in order to become actual, must be mediated by the phantasms, or imaginative forms, which lie halfway between intelligible and sensible forms. Without rejecting this interpretation of Aristotle, from which the above-mentioned philosophers inferred that the Active Intellect is a separate or transcendent power, St. Thomas argues that it is "still necessary to assign to the human soul some power of participation in that superior intellect, by which power the human soul makes things to be actually intelligible."[42] Although by that 'superior

---

37. *Summa Theologica.* I, Q. 79, a. 3. Resp. Cf. Q. 15, a. 3. Plato actually described the process of cognition as a mode of reminiscence, whereby the soul which pre-existed in the higher world is made to remember the Ideas with which it was originally conversant. Cf. *Phaedo*, 100.
38. *De Anima* III, 430a 15.
39. *Republic* VI, 508.
40. *De Anima* III, 430a 13.
41. *Summa Theologica* I, Q. 79, a. 4. Resp.
42. *Ibid.*, a. 5 and a. 1.

intellect' one would assume that St. Thomas meant transcendent, he appears in *Summa Contra Gentiles* to balk at this result. Referring to Aristotle's comparison of the Active Intellect to light, he comments that the

> disposition whereby the created intellect is raised to the intellectual vision of the divine substance is rightly called the light of glory; not indeed because it makes the object actually visible, as the light of the agent intellect does, but because it makes the intellect able to understand actually.[43]

In this respect, the Active Intellect's own light may be said to derive ultimately from the divine light, or 'light of glory.' For "the separate intellect, according to the teaching of our Faith" he writes, "is God Himself."[44]

His other reason for refusing to recognize the separability or transcendence of the Active Intellect and possible intellect alike is his already established thesis that they are both parts of the soul. Commenting on Aristotle's statement in *De Anima* III, 430a 18 that the agent is nobler than the patient, he argues that "the possible intellect is said to be separate, because it is not the act of any corporeal organ," and the same may be said about the Active Intellect, which is "called separate, but not as a separate substance"[45] – identified with the view of Avicenna which he explicitly rejects – but rather as immaterial.

Avicenna, it will be recalled, regarded the Active Intellect as the last of the series of intellects, or separate substances, which emanate from the One or Necessary Being. Commenting on this view and the manner in which intelligible forms (or species, as he calls them) flow into our souls, Aquinas writes: "Avicenna, setting this opinion [of Aristotle] aside, held that the intelligible species of all sensible things, instead of subsisting in themselves without matter, pre-exist immaterially in some separate intellects.[46] The separate intellect in which those 'species' or forms subsist is identified as the Active Intellect and Avicenna's view is contrasted with

---

43. *S. Cont. Gent.* III, ch. 53. Here St. Thomas quotes Pss. XXXV:10 and CIII:2; Isa. LX:19 and I John I:5.
44. *Summa Theologica.* I, Q. 79, a. 4. Resp. Cf. Q. 90, a.3, quoting Ps. IV:7.
45. *Ibid.,* I, Q. 79, a. 5, and a. 1.
46. *Ibid.,* I, Q. 84, a. 4. Resp.

that of Plato, who believed that the intelligible forms, or Ideas, subsist by themselves in the World of Ideas, but not in the Active Intellect, as Avicenna actually held, nor in the First Reason (Nous), as Plotinus held. From the Active Intellect, adds St. Thomas, Avicenna held that the intelligible forms flow into our souls, whereas sensible forms or species flow into corporeal matter.[47]

St. Thomas next turns to the question of the unity of the Active Intellect; and perhaps by analogy to the possible intellect, which, as we have seen, was the target of his attack on the Averroists, he denies that this intellect could be one and the same for all men. His chief argument is that, as a power of the soul, this intellect must be multiplied according to the number of individual souls. However, he does not deny that in a sense, this Active Intellect is common to all mankind, in so far as they enjoy in common the power to apprehend the first principles of demonstration, from which he concludes that the "possession of all men in common of first principles proves the unity of the *separate intellect*, which Plato compares to the sun, but not the unity of the agent intellect, which Aristotle compares to light."[48]

However, St. Thomas is categorical that by separate intellect should be understood, as we have seen earlier, God Himself, whose light illuminates the human mind, both in its possible and active capacities, enabling it thereby to apprehend the first principles of cognition which Aristotle regarded in *Analytica Posteriora* 1, 2, as the foundation of all genuine knowledge (*episteme*). The power to apprehend these first principles, which are innate, is, in short, the product of divine illumination or the 'light of glory' (*lumen gloriae*), rather than the overflowing of these principles from a supermundane agency, lying halfway between God and man, as Avicenna held. It was ultimately on this last thesis, in which Averroes and the Arab Neoplatonists generally concurred, that the thesis of the unity of the Active Intellect was predicated, and against which St. Thomas violently reacted. His intent, in the last analysis, may be said to have been the desire

---

47. *Ibid.* In *al-Najāt*, the abridgement of *al-Shifa*, p. 216, Avicenna describes the Active Intellect as the 'locus' (*mahall*) or storehouse of intelligible forms, as well as corporeal forms (p. 317) which flow into material entities, once they are 'disposed' to receive them.
48. *Ibid.*, I, Q. 79, a. 5, ad. 3. Cf. *S. Cont. Gent.* II, ch. 78.

to restore to knowledge its genuine and specific human character. W. D. Ross has commented on the view that the possible (passive) and active intellects (reasons) fall within the soul, to which he himself inclines, as follows: "This is fatal to any interpretation which identifies the active reason with a divine reason falling entirely outside the individual human being. It is not fatal to the view that the active reason is a divine reason immanent in human souls,"[49] which corresponds essentially to St. Thomas's own interpretation. The Active Intellect is a light within the human soul, whereby it participates in the divine light and is consummated by it, so to speak, whenever it apprehends the first principles of knowledge.

The Eternity of the World

Another major issue around which controversy raged throughout the Middle Ages, between Aristotle's followers and their adversaries, was the eternity of the world. Aristotle had in *Physics* VIII asserted that it is impossible that time could have a beginning, since that would mean that there was a time when time was not. In addition, time being the measure of motion, it follows that, like time, motion is eternal too.[50] In *Metaphysics* XII, he argues, substances are the first existing things. Now, if substances are "all destructible, all things are destructible."[51] This would entail that time and movement are destructible, in the sense of having a beginning and an end, which is absurd for the reasons already given. From the thesis of the eternity of time, motion and the movable (i.e., substance), Aristotle proceeds next to prove the existence of "something which is always moved with an unceasing motion, which is motion in a circle;"[52] that is, the first heaven or outermost sphere, and beyond it something which moves the first heaven while remaining unmoved; namely, the Unmoved Mover. Both the first heaven and the Unmoved Mover are then asserted to be eternal. In *Heavens* I, 179b 4 f., Aristotle reviews the opinions of his

---

49. Ross, *Aristotle*, p. 149.
50. Cf. *Physics* VIII, 251b 10 f., where Aristotle singles out Plato as the only philosopher who believed that time, together with the universe, had a beginning, as stated in *Timaeus*, 36B.
51. *Metaphysics* XII, 1071b 4 f.
52. *Ibid.*, 1071a 21.

predecessors, including Plato, Empedocles and Heraclitus, who believed the world to be generated, and therefore, to have had a beginning in time, against which he sets his own view of the eternity of time, motion and the movable, shared by Democritus and his school.

For Averroes, the eternity of the universe was equally unquestioned. In his *Large Commentary on the Metaphysics*, he asserts the absurdity of the doctrine of creation *ex nihilo* taught by the three religions prevalent in 'our time' (*tres leges quae hodie quidem sunt*), as the Latin translation has it.[53] This is reinforced in his 'theological' writings, including the *Tahāfut* and *al-Kashf*, by an array of arguments. Contrary to the claims of the Mutakallimun that the eternity of the world derogates from God's perfection or power, Averroes argues in these writings that it is rather the doctrine of creation in time that derogates from that power and perfection, by limiting God's action to one mode of production (i.e., creation in time), and reducing Him to a state of idleness or inactivity during the infinite lapse of time preceding the actual creation of the world.[54] Moreover, it raises the question of why God chose to create the world at that particular point in time and no other, a question referred to in the theological–philosophical controversies of the time as the problem of the eternal will. Al-Ghazālī and his fellow Ash'arites adhered to the view that God created the world in time through an act of 'eternal will' (*irādah qadīmah*);[55] to save God from the liability to change, consequent upon His willing at a specific point in time to bring the world into being. Averroes shows at length, as we have seen, the tenuousness of this view, which amounts to confusing the two concepts of will and action as predicated of God.

Continuous Creation or Creatio ab Aeterno

To circumvent the problems attendant upon creation in time, Averroes adheres to the thesis of eternal or 'continuous production' (*ihdāth dā'im*), as distinct from that of 'discontinuous production' (*ihdāth munqati'*),[56] which

---

53. Cf. *In Met.* XII (Venice 1552), fol. 143. Cf. Fakhry, "The Eternity of the World in Averroes, Maimonides and Aquinas," *Le Muséon*, p. 150.
54. Cf. *Tahāfut al-Tahāfut*, p. 162.
55. Cf. *Tahāfut al-Falāsifah*, pp. 26 f.
56. Cf. *Tahāfut al-Tahāfut*, pp. 96 f. and 162.

amounts to a partial concession to the Muslim protagonists of creation, without abandoning the Aristotelian thesis of eternity. The term he uses in this context is that of production or origination (*ihdāth*) rather than creation (*khalq*), which the Muslim philosophers generally steered clear of. Some, like Avicenna, opted for the term *ibdā'* (initiation), whereas al-Fārābī used the terms *ṣudūr* or *fayḍ* (emanation or overflowing). In the *Large Commentary on the Metaphysics*, Averroes uses another term, namely, *ījād*, meaning bringing into being and in *al-Kashf*, *ikhtirā'* or invention. In all these cases, the Muslim philosophers were clearly concerned to avoid the Qur'anic term *khalq*, which carried the double connotation of production *ex nihilo* and in time.

St. Thomas's view of eternity was at loggerheads with that of Averroes. However, without abandoning Aristotle's stand, he struggles valiantly with the *aporiae* raised in the *Physics* and *Metaphysics*, and, following the example of Maimonides, refers to Aristotelian texts, which appear to show that Aristotle had entertained certain doubts regarding the eternity of the world. Of these texts, the most explicit is Aristotle's statement in *Topica* I, 104b 16, which refers, in W. A. Picard-Cambridge's translation, to problems, "in regard to which we have no argument because they are so vast, and we find it difficult to give reasons; e.g., the question whether the universe is eternal or no."

Moreover, adds St. Thomas, in support of this thesis, Aristotle's arguments are not absolutely, but only relatively, demonstrative; these arguments being part of his polemic against his predecessors. For in both *Physics* VIII and *De Coelo* I, he premises some opinions, such as those of Anaxagoras, Empedocles and Plato, and brings forward arguments to refute them. Here St. Thomas notes that "whenever he (Aristotle) speaks of this subject, he quotes the testimony of the ancients, which is not the way of a demonstrator, but of one persuading of what is probable."[57]

According to scholarly opinion, heretofore, it was Maimonides who first referred in his *Guide of the Perplexed (Dux Perplexorum)* to those Aristotelian doubts regarding the eternity of the world,[58] as St. Thomas himself has acknowledged.

57. *Summa Theologica* I, Q. 46, a. 1. Resp.
58. Cf. *Dalālat* I, 73, p. 313 (Pines, p. 189).

However, Maimonides himself appears to have been continuing a Neoplatonic tradition, first referred to three centuries earlier by al-Fārābī in his *Reconciliation of Plato and Aristotle* (*al-Jam' bayna Ra'yay al-Ḥakīmayn*), which seems to have escaped the notice of scholars.[59] In that work, al-Fārābī cites the argument of Aristotle in *Topica*, according to which, as he has put it, "there are propositions with respect to which two contrary sides of an argument may be given, based on generally accepted premises; for instance, is the world eternal or not."[60] Such propositions, being dialectical, and given to illustrate a logical thesis, argues al-Fārābī, do not amount to demonstrations compelling conviction (*i'tiqād*). He then quotes Aristotle's statement, in *Heavens* I, 179a 7, that "the whole [i.e., universe] has no temporal beginning,"[61] from which some have supposed that Aristotle believed the world to be eternal. However, according to al-Fārābī, this is far from being the case, in so far as Aristotle had shown in the *Heavens*, as well as the physical and metaphysical treatises, that time is simply the measure of the motion of the spheres, "from which it is generated." Now, says al-Fārābī, "what is generated from a thing does not contain that thing." Aristotle's statement that the world has no temporal beginning, therefore, should be understood to mean "that it was not generated step by step together with its parts. For its parts preceded each other in time and time itself is generated by the movement of the sphere."[62] It follows, therefore, according to al-Fārābī, that it is impossible that the world should have a temporal beginning, and accordingly must have come into being "through the creative power (*ibdā'*) of God Almighty all at once and without time; and from its [i.e., the sphere's] movement time itself came into being."[63]

It is noteworthy that this explicit defense of the thesis of creation in time is in sharp contrast to al-Fārābī's well-known vindication of the contrary thesis of the eternal emanation of the universe from the First

---

59. S. Pines in his translation of the *Guide*, commenting on Maimonides' passing reference to Abū Nasr (al-Fārābī) writes: "The passage of al-Fārābī to which reference is made has not yet been identified" (p. 292).
60. Al-Fārābī, *al-Jam'*, in *Philosophischen Abhadlungen*, p. 22.
61. *Ibid.*, p. 22.
62. *Ibid.*, p. 23.
63. *Ibid.*

Being in the *Virtuous City* and elsewhere, and raises a crucial question regarding the authenticity of the *Reconciliation of Plato and Aristotle (al-Jam')*, on the one hand, and its ultimate Neoplatonic source, on the other. In the present state of our knowledge, the most important Neoplatonic document to have influenced the Arab–Islamic philosophers, from al-Kindī to al-Fārābī, Avicenna and Ṣadr al-Dīn al-Shirāzi is unquestionably the apocryphal *Theologia Aristotelis (Āthulogia)*, also known as 'the Book of Divinity.' This apocryphal treatise, repeatedly quoted by al-Fārābī in the *Reconciliation*, and upon which Avicenna is said to have written a commentary, was attributed to Aristotle in the Arabic sources, but is known today to have been a paraphrase of Plotinus' *Enneads* IV, V and VI, made probably by Porphyry of Tyre. This Porphyry, who was Plotinus' greatest disciple and his editor, is credited in the *Suidas* with a treatise entitled "That Plato's and Aristotle's Opinions are One."[64]

Here probably, like al-Fārābī, Porphyry was out to prove that the two great sages of antiquity could not have differed on essential questions, such as the eternity of the world, the existence of universals, vision, and so on; and in the process may have attempted to reconcile the Aristotelian view that the universe is eternal and the Platonic view, expressed in the *Timaeus*, that the universe was created in time out of formless matter, which Plato identified with the nothing, *to meon*. Al-Fārābī even refers to a treatise of Ammonius entitled the 'Demonstration of the Existence of the Maker *(Sāni')*,' which he says is too well-known to cite in this context.[65]

Hence, it appears that in this particular treatise, intended to prove that Plato and Aristotle were in total agreement on all major philosophical issues, al-Fārābī was simply continuing a Neoplatonic tradition which could not accept the notion that the two great sages were in serious disagreement on this important question of the eternity of the world.

Condemnation of Averroism, 1270 and 1277

Despite the enthusiasm with which Aristotle, as interpreted by Averroes, was received in learned circles in Paris in the second half of the thirteenth

64. Suidas, *Lexicon* II, 2, 373.
65. *al-Jam'*, in *Philosophischen Abhadlungen*, pp. 24 f.

century, serious questions began to be asked regarding the degree to which Aristotle's teaching in metaphysics and cosmology could be reconciled with Christian doctrine. In 1270, the Bishop of Paris, Etienne Tempier, issued a condemnation of fifteen propositions, of which thirteen were of Averroist inspiration. They included the unity of the intellect, the negation of free will, the eternity of the world, the mortality of the soul and the denial of divine providence.[66] This condemnation was followed in 1277, as mentioned earlier, by a papal bull, upon which Etienne Tempier based his new condemnation of 219 theses, which, although directed against the Latin Averroists, did not spare St. Thomas himself.[67] The pivotal point on which the two condemnations turned was the tendency of the new Aristotelian–Averroist current to consecrate the primacy of reason, at the expense of the primacy of faith. Some Latin Averroists, with Siger of Brabant and Boethius of Dacia at their head, were even suspected of subscribing to a double-truth theory, according to which a proposition may be true in philosophy but not true in theology and vice versa, without entailing any contradiction. St. Thomas, in *De Unitate Intellectus, Contra Averroistas*, confirms this suspicion, by attacking in vehement terms some unnamed contemporary, no doubt an Averroist, to whom he attributes the proposition, that "through reason, I conclude necessarily that the intellect is numerically one, But I firmly hold the opposite view by faith."[68] Averroes himself never really subscribed to such a theory and it is doubtful, according to Gilson and other medievalists, that Siger himself did so; but it is certain that St. Thomas was referring to some Latin Averroist in Paris whose name he did not wish to disclose.

The Three Levels of Assent (tasdīq)

For Averroes, as already mentioned in this study, the primacy of reason is unquestioned and it is for this reason that Gilson regards him as the herald of rationalism long before the Renaissance.[69] Averroes had in fact distinguished between three levels of assent (*tasḍīq*), the philosophical, the

---

66. Cf. Gilson, *La philosophie au moyen âge*, p. 558, and Mandonnet, *Siger de Brabant*, p. 111.
67. Gilson, *La philosophie au moyen âge*, p. 559.
68. *Aquinas Against the Averroists*, p. 143.
69. Cf. *Reason and Revelation*, pp. 37 f.

dialectical and the rhetorical. The first, which ensues upon the 'demonstration' of the philosophers, is higher than that of the theologians, or people of dialectic (*jadaliyūn*), or that of the masses at large, or the people of rhetoric (*khatābiyūn*), as he states in his *Decisive Treatise on the Relation of Philosophy and Religion (Faṣl al-Maqāl)*. In that 'theological' treatise, which was not available to St. Thomas, Siger of Brabant or their Latin contemporaries, Averroes maintains a position which may be called the 'parity' of truth, philosophical and religious. According to this position, philosophical truth, although superior to religious truth, is not really incompatible with it, or even different from it. The only difference between the two types of truth is that they are addressed to three different classes of hearers (or readers), and are for that reason cast in different idioms. In the event of 'apparent' conflict between the religious texts (in this case the Qur'an) and philosophical texts, chiefly Aristotle's, it is the duty of the philosophers, whom the Qur'an calls 'those who are well grounded in knowledge' (3:5–6), according to Averroes' own reading, to resolve the conflict by recourse to the method of interpretation (*ta'wīl*). This method had been consecrated by many accredited scholars. Properly understood and applied, the method of interpretation is bound to show that on all fundamental issues, philosophy (*hikmah*) is in agreement with religion (*sharīʿah*). However, neither the theologians nor the masses at large, warns Averroes, are qualified to undertake this kind of interpretation, only the philosophers or 'people of demonstration' are – a thesis which he illustrates in great detail in the above-mentioned treatise.[70] Here, he shows that neither on the question of eternity of the world, God's knowledge of particulars or bodily resurrection, which formed the brunt of al-Ghazālī's anti-philosophical polemic, are the pronouncements of the Qur'an unequivocal, in such a way as to justify the charge of infidelity (*kufr*) leveled at the philosophers. In fact, argues Averroes, if the inner meaning of Qur'anic passages is thoroughly probed, the position of the philosophers is found to be in agreement with that of the theologians, since the former are far from denying the creation of the world or the resurrection of the body. In the first case, the philosophers hold, as we

70. Cf. Fakhry, "Philosophy and Scripture in the Theology of Averroes," *Mediaeval Studies*, pp. 78–89.

have seen, that of the two modes of 'generation,' the continuous (*dā'im*), favored by the philosophers, and the discontinuous (*munqati'*), favored by the theologians, the former is more appropriately attributed to God. In the second case, the philosophers recognize that "the fact (*wujūd*) of resurrection is something that religions, in general, concur in and the demonstrations of the learned have established."[71] They only differ with respect to its mode (*sifah*), and whether it is really corporeal or spiritual. That is why, we find, states Averroes, that "all religious creeds are in agreement that souls will partake after death of certain conditions, either of bliss or misery. They only differ regarding the mode of representing these conditions and the manner of enabling mankind to understand them."

The 'sensuous representations' used in our religion (i.e. Islam), Averroes adds, "is more accessible to the majority of people and more likely to move their souls towards what exists beyond [i.e., in the Hereafter]."[72] However, 'spiritual representation,' although less effective in moving the souls of the masses, "is more acceptable to the people who engage in discourse and disputation and are but a minority,"[73] and who undoubtedly included the philosophers, according to Averroes.

With respect to the third charge which al-Ghazālī had leveled at the philosophers and which was debated in Scholastic circles in Paris and elsewhere;[74] namely, their denial of God's knowledge of particulars, Averroes takes an extremely subtle line, as we saw earlier. The whole controversy turns, according to him, on the proper understanding of the manner in which knowledge is predicated of God and of man. Al-Ghazālī and the Mutakallimun in general misunderstand this point and, therefore, predicate knowledge of God and man univocally. It should be clearly understood, however, that the two modes of knowledge, the human and divine, are entirely different; for God's knowledge is the cause of the object known (*ma'lūm*), whereas our knowledge is the effect (*ma'lūl*) and accordingly changes constantly in accordance with the changes which its

71. *Al-Kashf*, p. 240.
72. *Ibid.*, p. 244.
73. *Ibid.*, p. 144.
74. This was one of the 219 propositions condemned in 1277, by the Bishop of Paris, Etienne Tempier. Cf. Mandonnet, *Siger de Brabant*, I, p. 111, and II, p. 178.

object undergoes. God's knowledge, contrariwise, is unchangeable and cannot be described either as universal or particular, but is *sui generis*.[75] Its mode, like that of His will, Averroes states in the *Tahāfut*, is really unknowable to us and is known only to God.[76]

It is noteworthy that, in grappling with God's knowledge of particulars, St. Thomas arrives at a similar conclusion; in knowing Himself as the Cause or First Principle of created entities, God knows all things; or as he has put it in his commentary on the *Metaphysics*, "cum igitur a primo principio, quod est Deus . . . patet quod Deus cognoscendo seipsum, omnia cognoscit."[77] Therein lies the answer of both Averroes and Aquinas to Aristotle's claim in *Metaphysics* XII, 1074b 26 that it does not become the Unmoved Mover to think of anything inferior to itself. For, "are there not some things about which it is incredible that it should think?"[78], he asks rhetorically in an attempt to spare God the indignity of idle curiosity about the world beneath Him and safeguard thereby the utter transcendence of the activity of thought, which is, according to him, the very essence of God.

75. Cf. *Large Commentary on Metaphysics.* III, pp. 1707 f.
76. Cf. *Tahāfut al-Tahāfut,* p. 446.
77. *In Met.* XII, lect. xi.
78. *Metaphysics* XII, 1074b 15.

Conclusion

This study has shown, it is hoped, that Averroes was a towering figure in the history of philosophy in general and Aristotelianism in particular, both in the East and West. Surpassing all of his predecessors, from Alexander of Aphrodisias in the second century, to Boethius in the fifth century and Avicenna in the eleventh, he was the most meticulous expositor of Aristotle's philosophy in any language or clime, up to his own day. Despite his divergences from most of the early Greek or Arab commentators, whom he constantly refers to or criticizes, his understanding of the Master is profound. Thus, if we assess, for example, his conception of the Aristotelian scheme of the sciences, we are struck at once by his firm grasp of the coherence of the whole scheme. This was due in part to his desire to give a comprehensive account of the whole Aristotelian corpus in the form of paraphrases, middle or large commentaries of that corpus as we have seen. No wonder Averroes' approach to the various sciences on which those commentaries and paraphrases turned was thoroughly integrated. Thus, more explicitly than Aristotle himself, he regarded the study of logic as a necessary propaedeutic to the study of physics, and by extension the other sciences, including metaphysics and ethics. This formed for him part of the discursive method of deduction (*qiyās*), which he applies even to theology and jurisprudence. Moreover, in consonance with the Arabic and Syriac traditions, he went so far as to include rhetoric and poetics in the logical scheme, in apparent divergence from Aristotle himself, referred to in the Arabic sources sometimes as the Master of Logic (*Ṣāḥib al-Manṭiq*). However, he follows Aristotle's lead in regarding psychology as part of the science of physics, despite the Platonic and Neoplatonic protestations to the contrary. The practical sciences, for him, consisted of two parts, ethics and politics, whose interrelations are systematically delineated in his paraphrase of the *Republic* of Plato. As for theology (*kalām*), he clearly regarded it as amenable to philosophical or logical treatment in a way which was fairly alien to his predecessors, such as al-Fārābī and Avicenna, who kept off theological enquiry altogether. Even jurisprudence (*fiqh*) is integrated into the philosophical scheme, through the application of logical methodology in the form of rational deduction (*qiyās 'aqlī*), which he believed to be analogous to juridical deduction (*qiyās fiqhī*), as we have seen in the course of this study. The only part of the scheme of the sciences on which he has not dwelt in any great detail is mathematics, with the exception of astronomy. In that respect, too, he remains thoroughly Aristotelian.

Averroes' standing in the history of Islamic philosophy, of which his thought marks an epoch-making summation or synthesis, as we have seen, is unique, despite the criticisms and denigrations to which he was subjected by his own countrymen. In the first place, as I have tried to show, he outstripped his Muslim predecessors in two respects, (a) the precise definition of the relation of philosophy and religion (*sharī 'ah* or *shar'*) in a series of writings which have no parallel in Arabic philosophical or theological literature, and (b) the contribution to juridical enquiry, which had not been attempted by any of his predecessors among the philosophers. His thoroughness in reviewing the legal opinions of leading scholars, from Mālik to Abū Ḥanīfah, is sometimes reminiscent of his thoroughness in the analysis or discussion of Aristotelian texts.

Notwithstanding, his fate in the Muslim world was far from being felicitous. Even during his lifetime, as we have seen, he was suspected of heresy or irreligion (*kufr*), sent into exile and his books committed to the flames. His own countryman, the Cordovan Ibn 'Arabī (d. 1240), the great mystic, either misunderstood or deliberately distorted his thought, following one of their casual encounters. After a cryptic exchange, in which they simply uttered a solitary yes and no, Ibn 'Arabī claimed that they were in perfect agreement on the possibility of mystical experience, with which we know that Averroes had no sympathy. In confirmation of this claim, Ibn 'Arabī even puts in Averroes' mouth these words: "Glory be to God who has accorded me the personal favor of seeing one of those men who [see] with my eyes,"[1] by whom Ibn 'Arabī obviously meant himself.

Not only Ibn 'Arabī, but his own disciple, the mystic Ibn Sab'īn (d. 1270), was particularly scathing in his comments on Averroes' philosophical output. He lambasts him as "merely an imitator of Aristotle," adding that "he was a man of limited scope, faint understanding, foolish conceptions and lacking in intuition."[2] His most vehement critic, however, in the next century, was the Syrian Ibn Taymiyah (d. 1328), who reacted violently against the use of all the methods of proof, whether theological or philosophical, and went so far as to question the very foundations of Aristotelian logic in his *Refutation of the Logicians* (*al-Radd 'alā al-Mantiqiyyīn*). In another treatise, *al-'Aql wa'l-Naql* (*Reason and Tradition*), Ibn Taymiyah attacks Averroes for limiting the number of schools of *kalām* in his *al-Kashf* to four: the esoterics (*bātiniyah*), the literalists (*hashwiyah*), the Mu'tazilite and the Ash'arite, to the exclusion of the 'pious ancestors' (*al-salaf al-sālih*), "whose creed is the best creed of this [Muslim] community till the Day of Resurrection,"[3] as he puts it.

As for Averroes' impact on Western-European thought, the translation of the whole Averroist corpus of commentaries on Aristotle into Hebrew and Latin, starting early in the thirteenth century, had a far-reaching effect on philosophical and theological developments, as we have seen, throughout the next three centuries and beyond. The number of these translations was impressive. Harry A. Wolfson has estimated that these commentaries totaled thirty-eight of which Michael the Scot, Hermann

---

1. *Al-Futūhāt al-Makkiyah*, I, pp. 153 f. Cf. Corbin, *Le Soufisme d'Ibn 'Arabī*, p. 39.
2. *Budd al-'Ārif*, p. 143.
3. *Majmū' al-Rasā'il* I, p. 160.

the German and William de Lunis have translated fifteen into Latin.[4] On the basis of the inventory he has drawn up, he has concluded that of the thirty-eight titles, twenty-eight are extant in Hebrew, fifteen in Arabic characters, four in both Arabic and Hebrew and nine in Hebrew characters only. In 1962, a complete reprint of the Latin commentaries was published by Minerva Publications, Frankfurt, Germany in eleven volumes. This reprint, entitled *Opera Aristotlis cum Averrois Cordubensis Commentariis*, was based on the 1562–74 Venice edition, known as the Junta.

In modern times, the revival of interest in Averroes and his philosophy dates back to the publication by Ernest Rénan in 1852 of *Averroès et l'averroïsme*, which covered the whole range of subjects Averroes dealt with, as well as his reception in Hebrew and Latin circles in the thirteenth century and beyond. Since that time, European scholars, like M. J. Müller, L. Gauthier, Max Horten, S. Van den Bergh, M. Bouyges, M. Cruz Hernandez, O. Leaman and others, have edited, translated or commented on Averroes' various philosophical and theological writings.

In the Arab World, Farah Antūn (d. 1922) published in 1903 a book entitled *Ibn Rushd and his Philosophy* (*Ibn Rushd wa Falsafatuh*) dedicated, as he says in the preface, to the "new breed of reasonable men," who have understood that the root of all the ills of the East is "the mixing of worldly affairs with religion." The only remedy for these ills, according to him, is "absolute respect for freedom of thought and expression," whose chief warrant is the separation of religion from politics. In the course of the heated controversy which this book ·sparked off, Antūn proceeded to defend secularism in very eloquent terms. He appears to link this secularism to Averroist rationalism, as Dante had done centuries earlier, although it is not clear whether he was conversant with Dante's arguments in *De Monarchia*, discussed in an earlier chapter of this study.

Be this as it may, the publication of *Ibn Rushd and his Philosophy*, inspired in some respects by Rénan's *Averroès et l'averroïsme*, was at once the subject of controversy, led by Muḥammad 'Abduh (d. 1905), then

---

4. See "Revised Plan for Publication of a Corpus Commentariorum Averrois in Aristotelem," *Speculum* 38, pp. 90 f.

Grand Mufti of Egypt. That controversy centered on the question of rationalism and secularism which, as just mentioned, were the primary preconditions of progress in the East, according to Antūn. Muḥammad 'Abduh challenged this claim and argued that Islam was not averse, on the one hand, to rationalism, which was of the essence of Islam, and on the other, secularism, which was inimical to the 'global' view of life. This global view, 'Abduh held, was the mark of the superiority of Islam over other religions which call for the separation of the spiritual and the temporal, as in Christianity. That globalism (*shumūl*) has been defended by a variety of leading Arab and Muslim scholars in recent years, such as A. M. al-'Aqqād, S. Qutb, and A. A. Mawdūdi, and is one of the current slogans of Muslim fundamentalism. By contrast, a number of Arab intellectuals, such as M. 'Amārah, T. Tizayni and H. Muruwwah, have gone so far in their interpretation of Averroes as to regard him as one of the early forerunners of (Marxist) dialectical materialism and secularism.

Further instances of the revival of interest in Averroes in the Arab world are the numerous publications and editions of his works by such scholars as 'U. Amīn, A.-R. Badawi, F. Ahwāni, M. Qāsim, G. Anawāti and G. Jihāmi, as the Bibliography will show.

Select Bibliography

I. Averroes' Works (Arabic)

Bidāyat al-Mujtahid wa-Nihāyat al-Muqtasid, ed. A. M. Mu'awwad and A. A. 'Abd al-Mawjūd, Beirut, 1996.

Fasl al-Maqāl, ed. A. Nader, Beirut, 1961.

"Jawāmi' al Kawn wa'l-Fasād" in *Ras ā'il Ibn Rushd. Jawāmi' al-Samā al Tabī'i*, ed. M. Puig, Madrid 1983.

Al-Kashf 'an Manāhij al-Adillah, ed. M. Qasim, Cairo, 1961.

Kitāb al-Samā' al-Tabī'i (Jawāmi'), ed. J. Puig, Madrid, 1983.

Al-Kulliyāt fi'l-Tibb, ed. S. Shayban and A. al-Talibi, Cairo, 1989.

Rasā'il Ibn Rushd, Dā'irat al-Ma'ārif, Hyderabad, 1947.

Rasā'il Ibn Rushd al-Tibbiyah, ed. G. S. Anawati and S. Zayid, Cairo, 1987.

Risālat al-Ittisāl bi'l-'Aql al-Fa''āl, Appendix, *Talkhīs Kitāb al-Nafs*, ed. F. al-Ahwāni (see below).

Tafsīr mā Ba'd al-Tabī'ah, ed. M. Bouyges, Beirut, 19, 1938–52.

Tahāfut al-Tahāfut, ed. M. Bouyges, Beirut, 1930.

Talkhīs al-Āthar al-'Ulawiyah, ed. J. D. al-Alawi, Beirut, 1994.

Talkhīs Kitāb al-Hiss wa'l -Mahsūs, ed. H. Blumberg, Cambridge, Mass., 1972.

Talkhīs Kitāb al-Kawn wa'l-Fasād, ed. S. Kurland, Cambridge, Mass., 1958.

Talkhīs Kitāb al-Khatābah, ed. M. S. Salim, Cairo, 1971.

Talkhīs Kitāb al-Maqūlat, ed. M. Bouyges, Beirut, 1932.

Talkhīs Kitāb al-Nafs, ed. G. Nogales, Madrid, 1985.

Talkhīs Kitāb al-Nafs ed. F. al-Ahwāni, Cairo, 1950 (includes *Risālat al-Ittisāl bi'l-'Aql al-Fa''āl*).

Talkhīs Kitāb al-Shi'r, ed. Ch. Butterworth and A. Haridi, Cairo, 1986.

Talkhīs Mā Ba'd al-Tabī'ah, ed. U. Amin, Cairo, 1958.

Talkhīs Mantiq Aristu, ed. G. Jihāmi, Beirut, 1982.

II. Translations and References

al-'Alawi, J. D. *Al-Matn al-Rushdi*, al-Dar al-Bayda', 1986.

Aquinas, St. Thomas, *Aquinas Against the Averroists*, trans. R. McIneny, West Lafayette, IN: Purdue University Press, 1993.

Aquinas, St. Thomas, *On Being and Essence*, trans. A. Maurer, Toronto: Pontifical Institute of Mediaeval Studies, 1968.

Aquinas, St. Thomas, *Summa Contra Gentiles*, trans. English Dominican Fathers, London: Burns, Oates & Washbourne, 1928.

Aquinas, St. Thomas, *Summa Theologica*, ed. Anton C. Pegis, New York: Modern Library, 1948.

Asín Palacios, *Ibn Massura y su escuela*, Madrid: Libros Hiperion, 1992.

Averroes, *In Moralia Nicomachea Expositione*, Venice, 1562.

Averroes on de Substantia Orbis (Hebrew and English), ed. A. Hyman, Cambridge, MA.: Mediaeval Academy of America and Jerusalem: Israel Academy of Sciences and Humanities, 1986.

Averroes on Plato's "Republic", trans. R. Lerner, Ithaca and London: Cornell University Press, 1974.

Averroes on the Harmony of Religion and Philosophy, trans. G. Hourani, London: Luzac & Co., 1961.

Averroes, *The Incoherence of the Incoherence*, trans. S. Van den Bergh, London, 1996.

Averrois Cordubensis Commentarium Magnum in Aristotelis De Anima Libros, ed. F. S. Crawford, Cambridge, MA.,: Mediaeval Academy of America, 1953.

Booth, E., *Aristotelian Aporetic Ontology in Islamic and Christian Thinkers*, Cambridge, Cambridge University Press, 1983.

Burrel, D., "Aquinas's Attitude towards Avicenna, Maimonides and Averroes," *The Cambridge Companion to Aquinas*, New York: Cambridge University Press, 1993.

Corbin, H., *Le Soufisme d'Ibn 'Arabi*, Paris: 1977.

Dante, Alighieri, *Monarchy and Three Political Letters*, trans. D. Nicholl, New York: 1955.

Endrell, G. and Aertsen, T. (eds.), *Averroes and the Aristotelian Tradition* (Proceedings of the Fourth Symposium on Averroism, Cologne, 1996), Leiden: Brill, 1999.

Fakhry, M., *A History of Islamic Philosophy*, London and New York: Columbia University Press, 1983.

Fakhry, M., *Islamic Occasionalism and its Critique by Averroes and Aquinas*, London: Allen & Unwin, 1958.

Fakhry, M., "Philosophy and Scripture in the Theology of Averroes," *Mediaeval Studies*, Toronto, 30 (1968), pp. 139–155.

Fakhry, M., "The Eternity of the World in Averroes, Maimonides and Aquinas," *Le Muséon*, 1952.

Gauthier, L., *Ibn Rochd (Averroes)*, Paris: Presses Universitaires de France, 1948.

Gilson, E., *Being and Some Philosophers*, Toronto: Pontifical Institute of Mediaeval Studies, 1952.

Gilson, E., *La philosophie au moyen âge*, Paris: Payot, 1947.

Gilson, E., *Reason and Revelation in the Middle Ages*, New York: Charles Scribner's Sons, 1932.

Hernandez, M. C., *Ibn Ruśd (Averroes)*, Cordova: Obra Social y Cultural Cajasur, 1997.

Jolivet, J. (ed.), *Multiple Averroes*, Paris, Belles Lettres, 1978.

Kretzmann, N. et al., *The Cambridge History of Later Medieval Philosophy*, London and New York, Cambridge University Press, 1984.

Al-Kindī, *On First Philosophy*, trans. A. Ivry, Albany, NY: SUNY Press, 1974.

Leaman, O., *Averroes and his Philosophy*, Oxford: Clarendon, 1988.

Maimonides, M., *Guide of the Perplexed*, trans. S. Pines, Chicago: Chicago University Press, 1965.

Mandonnet, P., *Siger de Brabant et l'averroïsme Latin au XIII siècle*, Louvain: Institut superieur de philosophie de l'Universite, 1908–11.

Pine, M. L., *Pietro Pompanazzi, Radical Philosopher of the Renaissance*, Padua: Antenore, 1986.

Rahman, F., "Essence and Existence in Avicenna," *Medieval and Renaissance Studies*, London: Warburg Institute, 1958.

Rénan, E., *Averroès et l'averroïsme*, Paris: Michel Lévy Frères, 1882.

Ross, W. D., *Aristotle*, London: Methuen, 1956.

Sarton, G., *Introduction to the History of Science*, Baltimore: Carnegie Institute of Washington, 1947, 1950 (reprint).

Wolfson, H., "Revised Plan for the Publication of a Corpus Commentariorum Averrois in Aristotelem," *Speculum*, 38, (1963), pp. 88–104.

The Qur'an, a Modern English Version, trans. M. Fakhry, Reading: Garnet Publishing, 1998.

III. Arabic Sources

Anawati, G. S., *Mu'allafāt Ibn Rushd*, Algiers: 1978.

Antūn, Farah, *Ibn Rushd wa Falsāfuh*, Beirut: 1988.

Al-Ash'ari, *Maqālat al-Islamiyin*, ed. H. Ritter, Istanbul: 1930.

Al-Baghdadi, *Usūl al-Din*, ed. H. Ritter, Istanbul: 1928.

Al-Fārābī, *Deux ouvrages inédits sur la rhétorique*, ed. J. Langhade and M. Grignaschi, Beirut: Dār al-Mashriq, 1971.

Al-Fārābī, *Al-Jam' bayna Ra'yay al-Hakīmayn*, in *Philosophischen Abhandlungen*, ed. F. Dieterici, Leiden: 1890.

Al-Fārābī, *Kitāb al-Hurūf*, ed. M. Mahdi, Beirut: Dar al-Mashriq, 1970.

Al-Ghazālī, *Tahāfut al-Falāsifah*, ed. M. Bouyges, Beirut: Imprimerie Catholique, 1927.

Ibn Abi Usaybi'ah, A., *'Uyūn al-Anbā'*, ed. N. Rida, Beirut: Dar Maktabat 'al-Hayah, 1965.

Ibn 'Arabi, *Al-Futūhāt al-Makkiyah*, I, Cairo: AH 1329.

Ibn Khaldūn, *Al-Muqaddimah*, Beirut: n. d.

Ibn Sab'īn, *Budd al-'Ārif*, Beirut: 1978.

Ibn Sīnā, *Al-Ishārāt wa'l-Tanbihāt*, ed. J. Forget, Leiden: 1892.

Ibn Sīnā, *Kitāb al-Najāt*, ed. M. Fakhry, Beirut: Dar al-Afaq al-Jadidah, 1985.

Ibn Taymiyah *Majmū' al-Rasā'il*, I, Cairo: 1905.

Ibn Tūmart, M., *A'azz mā Yutlab*, ed. A. al-Talibi, Algiers: 1985.

Al-Kindī, *Fi'l-Falsafah al-Ūla*, ed. A. H. Abu Rida, Cairo: 1948.

Maimonides, M., *Dalalat al-Ḥa'irin*, ed. H. Atay, Istanbul: 1981.

Al-Marākushi, M., *Al-Mu'jib fi Talkhīs Akhbār al-Maghrib*, Leiden: E. J. Brill, 1881.

Ṣā'id Ibn Ṣā'id, al-Andalusi, *Tabaqāt al-Uman*, ed. L. Sheikho, Beirut: 1912.

Index